H**A**PPINESS

...AS A SECOND LANGUAGE

A Guidebook to Achieving
Lasting, Permanent Happiness

By Valerie Alexander

This book is also available on the World Wide Web as an eBook.
Visit www.SpeakHappiness.com for details.

Author Photo by Samantha Ronceros
Cover Design by Valerie Alexander
Cover Layout by Joshua Barragan
Internal Page Design and Layout by Ramesh Kumar Pitchai

Hello and welcome to Happiness as a Second Language!

You can read this book over the course of a day, or over the course of a lifetime. I recommend the latter.

It will be easy to blow past the first few chapters; to think they don't apply to you. They do. You might be tempted to dismiss this book as trite or silly after reading about using your favorite color to change your mood without ever actually trying it. Please don't.

Your journey is not a sprint. It's not even a marathon. It's a trek that will take weeks, months or maybe even years. You can do it on your own and have incredible results, or you can join fellow travelers also seeking to learn this awesome new language, Happiness.

You'll be amazed at the difference the slow and steady approach makes, and how much easier the work in the later chapters will be once you've laid the groundwork.

If you think it would benefit you, find others and form a club. Do all of the exercises together, and report to one another on your progress. Commit to work through each chapter – maybe one a week or one a month, whatever works for you. Cheer each other on!

For book clubs, please don't make this your selection for a single week then move on. Make it the "B-story" that you come back to for a few minutes each week, continuously over the course of a season.

Not everything in this book is for everyone. I know that. But more of it is for you than you might think. Give it all a shot. Find what works and keep at it.

If you read this book today, you won't be instantly fluent in Happiness tomorrow. If you read this book to change, you will meet success you never imagined, and soon enough, Happiness will be your native language. I promise.

Happily,
Valerie

TABLE OF CONTENTS

FOREWORD

MY EVOLUTION INTO HAPPINESS

February 11, 2000 was the worst day of my life. When people hear the story, most of them think it's not possible that all of it happened on the same day, but it did. I started the day in a restaurant in Honolulu and ended it in a hospital in Louisville, Kentucky, never realizing that the events of that day would start me on a downward spiral that would end with a comically stupid attempt to end my own life six weeks later.

At the time, I was living outside San Francisco and working for a start-up tech company in Hawaii, which required me to spend the first week of every month in Honolulu. That sounds glamorous on the page, but the truth is, the inside of a conference room on Oahu can be just as grim as the inside of a conference room in Omaha – even more so when you spend 14 hours a day there and paradise is right outside the door.

Taking the 6:45 a.m. flight on the first Monday of each month, packing three weeks' worth of meetings into four and a half days, and returning on the 12:45 p.m. flight on Friday was becoming miserable. Worse, the company was proving to have less and less ability to execute our business plan with each passing month, and the CEO was becoming less and less patient, especially since it was mostly his money financing the thing.

That Friday morning in February, I woke up in Hawaii knowing it was going to be a rough day. As someone who is very bad at conflict, any situation that is guaranteed to be contentious is enormously difficult for me, and this one was gearing up to be a doozy.

I had scheduled a breakfast with the CEO to explain that I would be leaving the company at the end of the month. I struggled terribly with this decision. It was a small company, not doing particularly well, and there was no question that my departure was going to hurt them badly. Still, it was the necessary thing to do.

My boss did not take this news well. Much worse, in fact, than I could have possibly anticipated, and after a heated 45 minutes, I relented and agreed not only to stay with the company, but to spend more time in Hawaii – the part of the job I hated most. (Yes, I am that bad at conflict.)

After breakfast, I arrived at the Honolulu airport for my flight home when my cell phone rang. My sister was calling to tell me that our mother was in the hospital. Doctors had discovered a brain tumor the size of a navel orange, and they were going to operate as soon as possible. I called my boss and told him (which – to his credit – he handled beautifully), then made arrangements to take the red-eye from San Francisco to Louisville that night, giving me about three hours at home to repack and get my things in order. I didn't have to worry about the house or my dog, since my boyfriend lived with me, so the plan was simply to pack and go. Things didn't exactly work out that way.

❄❄❄

The prior November, my boyfriend had gotten the shock of his life – a letter from the State of Montana stating that there was a little girl on public assistance, and the state was going after the father for back child support. By January, DNA tests confirmed that this child was his (the result of a one-night stand he didn't even remember from eight years earlier), and he was facing some serious financial consequences.

I handled that news like a champ. How should we budget for the child support? Did he need me to find him a lawyer to fight the back support and penalties that the state intended to impose? Would we need to fight for custody, since the mother had emotional and substance abuse problems?

The only thing I asked in return was that we approach this little girl like a family: a cohesive parenting unit. I knew how a seven-year-old was going to see something like this. I was seven when my dad left.

I didn't want to seem like an interloper, or for her to have any illusions about Mommy and Daddy getting "back together." I wanted her to understand that I was not a roadblock to the perfect family she might have been dreaming of, but would be the other parent in any relationship she would have with her father. My boyfriend completely agreed with this entire strategy. At least, that's what he said.

❊❊❊

The night of Friday, February 11, 2000, I got home from Honolulu, on my way to Louisville, and my boyfriend was nowhere to be found. I called his office, then friends, co-workers, and finally his mother in Montana.

My heart sank when she told me he was there. It was the worst thing I could have heard. He'd gone to meet his daughter without me. The neighbors had been taking care of the dog while I was in Hawaii.

I didn't have time to process any of that. My flight was in two hours and now, at ten o'clock at night, I had to find a way to get to the airport with my 90-pound German shepherd and her giant crate. Thank God the flight was a red-eye, because that meant everyone was sleeping while I spent the next four hours crying my eyes out.

❋❋❋

Everything went smoothly with my mom's operation, and I returned on March 1st to California, where my first phone call was to the CEO in Hawaii to tell him I quit, and the second was to the boyfriend to tell him to get all his stuff out of my house. I then crawled into bed and didn't get up for three weeks.

As incomprehensible as this is in hindsight, at the time, all signs in the universe were telling me I was a failure. A complete, utter, total, worthless failure. I couldn't imagine how the world wouldn't be better off without me in it, so I started thinking about how I could end my life. If you have never experienced this level of depression, it is impossible to describe, but when you're in it, it's easy to convince yourself that you have nothing to live for, and everyone you love would be relieved if you were dead.

I finally decided that what I really wanted to do was drive down to Monterey, find a cliff above the rocks and just drive off. I grabbed my things to head out, when Jasmine, the German shepherd, hearing the car keys, tore out the door in front of me and sat by the car. Without thinking, I opened the back door and she hopped in.

Oakland to Monterey is a two-hour drive, but for the life of me, I can't remember a minute of it. I only remember finding the spot on the side of the cliff where I wanted to drive off. That's when I glanced in the rear-view mirror and discovered the dog was in the car. Crap.

"Well, I can't reward the most loyal creature on the planet by watching her fly past me through the windshield as I crash into the rocks," I thought. I opened the back door and made her get out. She seemed really confused to be on the side of Highway 1, and as a car whizzed by, I realized that leaving her there would not only get her killed, but also might kill the people who swerved to avoid her. I screamed. "Oh my God, I am so stupid!"

I put the dog back in the car, got in and drove home, sobbing the whole way. "Could I be a bigger failure?" I cried. "I can't even kill myself without screwing it up." I decided to try again the next day, but that night, my friend Shari called from New York to tell me that her husband, an attorney, had a trial in Reno and she was coming out with him to go skiing for the weekend. His law firm was paying for a suite at the hotel, and I was welcome to join them.

I said no, but she could tell that something wasn't right, so she pushed...and pushed...and pushed. She told me if I wouldn't come to Reno, then she'd just come down to see me instead. In short, she wouldn't get off the phone with me until I agreed to come.

So the next day, instead of driving back to my perfect cliffside suicide in Monterey, I put the dog in the kennel and drove to Reno.

I was a dud all weekend, but no one got that annoyed. Shari's friend Dave lived in Reno and he spent most of the weekend hanging out with us as well. Then, Monday morning, when Shari went off to ski and her husband went off to court, Dave and I headed down to the buffet at the Sterling Casino at 10:00 a.m. and stayed there until after nightfall.

We hung out and grazed through two waitress shifts as I told Dave (a complete stranger) what was going on – my job debacle, the loser boyfriend, mom's brain tumor and a million other things that painted a picture of a failure. A total failure. Nothing but a failure. He should be prepared to run, lest it be contagious.

Only here's the thing, Dave didn't see me as a failure. In fact, he thought I was kinda nifty, and he somehow convinced me to see myself that way.

After eight hours in the buffet (and a very healthy tip for the waitstaff), we went back to the room, I packed up and drove home. I thanked Dave and Shari for saving my life that weekend, but I don't think they ever knew (until now) how serious I was.

❋❋❋

Back in the Bay Area, I started looking for a new job. It was the height of the Internet boom and in the previous five years, I had been an IPO lawyer, a venture capital consultant, a tech-sector investment banker and an Internet executive, and in the spring of 2000, the whole world was open to me. In fact, as word got out in the venture community that I was looking for work, I was being offered jobs that I didn't even interview for.

Jobs were plentiful and anyone with a shred of experience was like a prize pig at the fair. Some of the offers were really tempting, but for some reason, they all sounded awful to me.

To this day, I cannot figure out what was compelling me to say no to everything, but something was. Then, on May 9, 2000, I got a call from my sister. That day, she had driven four hours from her home in Knoxville, Tennessee, to New Albany, Indiana, to pick up my mom and take her another two hours to a specialist in Cincinnati, then two hours back to Indiana and another four hours back to Knoxville, all with her four-year-old son in the car.

That night, I called three real estate agents. All three came over to bid for the listing. The house went on the market ten days later, we accepted bids ten days after that, then I sold my car, gave away all my furniture, rented a storage unit for everything else, and on July 7, 2000, got on a plane with two suitcases and the dog to spend the next 10 months doing nothing but hanging out with my mom. It was where I was needed. It was also exactly what I needed.

Just to clarify – I am not the daughter who changes bandages. I'm the daughter who hires the disability lawyer. I'm also the only person who was somehow able to convince my mother, who had been working since she was 14, that not having a job or a family to raise did not mean she had nothing to do.

We traveled all over the eastern seaboard that year, and I knew things were going to be fine in early 2001 when she said to me, "I hope I never have to go back to work."

Satisfied that she would be okay, I started looking at returning to California, only there was one problem. I had been an IPO lawyer, a venture capital consultant, a tech-sector investment banker and an Internet executive, and by the spring of 2001, ten months after the Internet bubble burst, those jobs no longer existed.

For the first time in my life, I had the luxury of making a choice based on what I really wanted, not what I needed or what was expected of me. The sale of my house paid off my student loans and gave me some breathing room when it came to income, so the decision was about where I wanted to live (anywhere in the world) and what career would make me happy (anything I could pay my bills doing). I decided I wanted to make movies.

I moved to Los Angeles, where I did not know a single person (other than a lawyer in Pasadena whose couch I camped on for three weeks), and gave myself two years to make it as a screenwriter.

One year and ten months later, I was sitting in Joel Schumacher's living room, pitching my "take" on a book adaptation he was going to direct for Phoenix Pictures, which became my first paid writing gig.

❋❋❋

February 11, 2000, was the best day of my life. That's the day that kicked me out of inertia and onto the path of choosing Happiness as my motivating force.

And here's the interesting thing: I've had a lot of ups and downs since that day. Success and failure in my chosen field. Relationships that ended in heartbreak and one that will last into eternity. Disloyal friends, untrustworthy business partners, the loss of my four-legged best friend, and the discovery of a wonderful new city, amazing people and the screwiest business I never imagined working in. And through it all, I've stayed happy.

I figured out that it's not my circumstances that make me happy, it's that I have to be a happy human being. It has to be who I am: my core. Like protecting my family or believing in God, that core must be unshakable.

Prior to February 11, 2000, I was not a happy person, but I am now. It's taken more than a decade to look back and see what steps I took to get here, and I hope that now I can somehow share with others what I've learned – both the hard way and the easy way.

This is not an afternoon read, but rather a textbook that will give you as much back as you put into it. Spend a few days or weeks on each chapter to see what works for you and what doesn't, and whatever you do, never give up on being happy. It is within your reach.

If you're reading this book, that means you've chosen to pursue happiness, and that's the most important step of all.

INTRODUCTION

How Do You Learn Happiness?

Was Greek spoken in your home as a child? If it wasn't, are you angry at your parents for not teaching you Greek? It's probably not their fault. I doubt Greek was spoken in their homes growing up, either.

When you left home to strike out on your own, did you start naturally speaking Greek? After all, if you wanted to speak Greek, wouldn't you just have to think really hard about it? Dwell on it until you were fluent? Couldn't you just decide you were ready to be a Greek speaker and the language would come to you? Doesn't learning a new language work that way?

It doesn't?

So if a particular language wasn't spoken in your home growing up, you probably wouldn't expect to know it by instinct. If you wanted to be a bona-fide Greek speaker, you would put a lot of time and effort into learning the language, step by step, part by part, until you were fluent. That's how you learn something foreign to you.

Which begs the questions:

Was Happiness practiced in your home as a child? Are you angry at your parents for not teaching you Happiness? It's probably not their fault. I doubt Happiness was in their homes growing up, either.

When you left home to strike out on your own, did you start naturally experiencing Happiness then? If you wanted Happiness, wouldn't you just have to think really hard about it? Dwell on it until you were "fluent?" Maybe you could just decide you were ready to be happy and Happiness would come to you. Doesn't it work that way?

No. It doesn't.

For most people, Happiness is as foreign a language as Greek. The difference is, we don't seem to think we have to learn Happiness. We expect it to come to us naturally, or believe that it will magically arrive when our circumstances change. In fact, we probably never think about it at all.

However, if Happiness is not your native language, then you have to teach yourself to "speak it," through the same steps you would take to teach yourself Greek.

This book is structured to make you fluent in Happiness by the last page. You'll learn how to introduce yourself as happy; how to count and to use the days of the week, months of the year, and all the colors in the rainbow. You'll learn the verbs, nouns and adjectives of Happiness; Happiness in the past, present, future and "future uncertain" tense; a few key phrases to help you navigate in your new language, and how to avoid the setbacks that happen when learning anything new.

Treat this as you would any other textbook. Do the exercises, follow the lessons, highlight, make notes, go back and recheck areas you may have forgotten or just need a refresher. More importantly, don't expect everyone else in your life to magically be proficient in Happiness simply because you are. You wouldn't expect that of them if you were learning Greek, would you? You're not responsible for anyone else's happiness, only your own. But that's the best place to start. The only place, really.

Believe me, you can be fluent in Happiness. It's easier than you think.

It's certainly easier than Greek.

CHAPTER

1

SAYING WHO YOU ARE

Je m'appelle Valerie
Me llamo Valerie
Il mio nome è Valerie

I have studied three foreign languages. I wish I could say that I am at least conversant in one of them, but sadly, these are skills that went by the wayside as more pressing issues of life were addressed. However, I still remember one important phrase from all of the languages I studied, and that is how to introduce myself – how to tell a complete stranger who I am.

It's the first thing you learn in a foreign language, as the teacher breezes into the room and announces, "Je m'appelle Madame Clarice." Of course, you thought she was crazy, but you knew right away that she'd just told you her name.

The same applies in learning Happiness. The first thing you need to learn how to say in this new language is, "I am happy." It doesn't have to be entirely accurate yet, but you do have to get used to saying it. Acceptable variations include, "I'm happy," "I'm a happy person," or if you text more than you speak, "I M HPPY."

You should probably not go around saying this to everyone you meet, but at least three or four times a day, say it to yourself. It's even more effective if you say it out loud. Try it now. Say, "I'm happy."

It's okay if this feels a little stupid, or even if it just doesn't feel right yet. You'll get more comfortable with this over time. If you want to accelerate your acceptance of this phrase, use it in the face of happiness challenges. In other words, announce your happiness to yourself in a moment of natural unhappiness.

Last week, I was driving down a very busy street and was stuck behind a man who was going rrrrreeeeaaaalllllyyyyy ssssllllloooooowwwwwlllyyyy. I have very little tolerance for this, especially when we missed a green light we both should have made. As I started to boil, I stopped and told myself (out loud, since I was alone in the car), "I'm a happy person."

The effect was quite surprising. As soon as I said it, I realized that happy people don't let one slow driver ruin their day. Happy people don't need to get where they're going at the speed of light, and most importantly, happy people don't scream out the window of their car at other drivers (I didn't do that, but believe me, I was close).

In fact, the one thing that stopped me from being completely miserable was reminding myself that I was happy, even though it wasn't true when I said it. Announcing that you are happy does not make it so, but it gets you closer, and it gets you *a lot* closer than announcing that you are unhappy...or screaming out the window at a total stranger.

ASSIGNMENT:

CHOOSE AT LEAST THREE times in your day when you will pause and say, "I'm happy." Try to arrange them around times that you are naturally happy, like when you leave work, or drop the kids off at school, or watch your favorite program on TV. Then, at least once a day, when you're feeling sad, angry, lonely, tired or frustrated, stop and remind yourself that you're happy. It won't make it so, but it will disrupt the signal in your brain that was making you unhappy.

A lot of the exercises in this book are about creating signal disruptors or signal boosters for your happiness. If you find yourself spiraling into unhappiness at any point during the day, think of a quick signal disruptor to change the direction your brain is going. Saying "I'm a happy person" is a great one. Many more follow in the next few chapters. The more you can boost your happiness, or disrupt your unhappiness, the easier you'll find it is to be happy.

Which leads to the next opportunity to introduce yourself in your new language of Happiness: when people ask how you are, instead of just saying, "Fine," try saying, "I'm happy." This is tricky, because it will always (Always!) lead to a follow-up comment or question. For this reason, pronunciation is very important, as is learning a few more key Happiness phrases for your first official conversation in your new language.

First, make sure that you know how to pronounce the word "happy" correctly when you reply. You do not want it to be a question:

"Hi, how are you?"

"I'm...happy?"

Ninety-nine percent of the time, answering like this elicits the response, "Really? You don't sound happy." You don't want this, because it automatically leads to a conversation in your native language, where you are either defending your happiness (something that is generally more stressful than it is convincing), or worse, expounding on your unhappiness, which will take you farther away from your goal.

You also don't want to sound overly enthusiastic.

"Hi, how are you?"

"I'm HAPPY!"

This will make most people take a step back and remove sharp objects from your vicinity. It also doesn't sound very convincing. When telling someone you're happy, you want to avoid sounding confused, tired, bored, angry or mentally unbalanced.

The next time you have a few minutes of peace and quiet, try this: create a complete visual image of yourself as a happy person. You have everything you want. You look the way you want to look. The people who you respect and admire, respect and admire you in return. The people you love, love you in return. Seriously, close your eyes and imagine this. Keep piling on the positive thoughts until a true and genuine smile crosses your face.

Now, out loud, still smiling, say, "I'm happy."

That's how you want to sound when people ask how you are.

Will that be the end of the conversation? Sadly, no.

"I'm happy," is not a response people expect, so you will get a variety of reactions that you need to be prepared for, ranging from suspicious to jealous to antagonistic. Just remember, you want to speak Happiness. Don't let someone else force you back into your native language (such as Insecurity, Defensiveness, Unworthiness, Anger, Sadness, Fear, or whatever was spoken principally in your home growing up).

On the following page are some of the possible conversations that can happen when you tell someone you're happy:

You say "I'm Happy." They say:	Your old reply (in your Native Language):	Your reply in Happiness (with a smile):
"Really?" (This is the most natural response. Regardless of their tone, reply as if there is no judgment attached to this question, just sincere curiosity.)	"No. Not really. But I'm reading this stupid book that says I'm supposed to say that. I sound like an idiot, don't I?"	"Yeah, really. Not 100% of the time, but more often than not. And I'm working on being happy all the time. It's nice. How are you doing?" (Changing the subject to them is a great way to preserve your happiness.)
They say:	**Your old reply:**	**Your Happiness reply:**
"Yeah, right."	"Don't be a jerk. I'm happy, dammit. Don't try to ruin that for me."	"No, I am. It's good. Hey, how's that thing at work you've been worried about?"
They say:	**Your old reply:**	**Your Happiness reply:**
"What are you so happy about?"	"I'm just happy, okay? It doesn't mean anything. I have a lot to be happy about. I'm not going to list it all for you here and now, but believe me, I am totally happy. Yeah. Totally."	"Just happy. Hey, did your mother ever get her test results back?"

They say:	Your old reply:	Your Happiness reply:
"God, I wish I could be happy."	"You can be. You just need to really focus on it. Learn how to speak Happiness as a Second Language. Introduce yourself as Happy. Really make it happen."	"Sorry to hear you say that. Is everything okay?"
They say:	Your old reply:	Your Happiness reply:
"That's so great!"	"Not really. I probably can't keep it up. You know me, always starting new things and giving up before I get anywhere."	"Thank you. How are you?"

Here is the most important thing to remember, when faced with skeptics: you will not change their minds, but you can change the subject – to them. This is what they'd rather be talking about anyway.

When someone is intent on challenging your happiness, try to remember something specific about them (their job, kids, family, last vacation, etc.) and ask about it. The conversation almost always will go in that direction and never get back to your mysterious happiness. This is good. You are just learning the language of Happiness yourself. Do not attempt to teach it to others. You're not ready yet and a lot gets lost in the translation.

ASSIGNMENT:

Next time someone asks, "How are you?" Reply, "I'm happy." Be prepared for the ensuing challenges. Smile, don't get knocked off your game, and as quickly as possible, change the subject to the other person. Once the encounter ends, walk away proud of yourself for your first real conversation in Happiness. Give yourself a little treat. Then, tomorrow, do it all over again.

CHAPTER

2

THE NUMBERS OF HAPPINESS

Uno, dos, tres, cuatro, cinco

Un, deux, trois, quatre, cinq

ichi, ni, san, shi, go

C an you count to five in at least one foreign language? Chances are very good that you can. Counting is one of those easy, rote memorization things that we all learn right away in a new language.

So how do you count in Happiness? It's a little different, but just as easy to learn. In Happiness, you count by making a list of five things that make you happy. Do this daily. Some things will appear on your list every day, and some things will be new from one day to the next.

There are a variety of techniques for counting to five in Happiness. You can wait until the end of the day and write down five things that come to mind. You can create categories and write one thing from each (for example, Today my children made me happy by...; Today, my job made me happy by...; Today, I made me happy by...) You can pick any moment in the day when you have a free minute and come up with five things on the spot.

Keep a small notebook with you at all times, and whenever something in your day makes you noticeably happy, whip it out and write it down. Warning: this often leads to lists longer than five.

I shared this with a friend who decided to keep paper and pens in every room in her house (even the bathroom!), and in her car and at her desk, just to write down her happy moments as soon as they occur to her. Her lists are funny, because she keeps track in her head of what number she's on and continues the sequence from place to place. In other words, she writes number one in the kitchen in the morning (1 - I'm happy the coffee tastes so good today); numbers two and three at work (2 - I'm happy that our company got that big contract; 3 - I'm happy that JoAnn broke up with her boyfriend so I won't have to keep hearing about their problems); number four in the car while waiting to pick up the kids from somewhere (4 - I'm happy Jason finally found a soccer team he likes); and number five in bed that night (5 - I'm happy we finally have a night that the heat doesn't have to be on). The pad in her bedroom is filled with only number five entries. I find this very amusing.

One of the early readers of this book said I should take out the part about my friend being "happy that JoAnn broke up with her boyfriend" because that was too negative and a turn-off, but if something like that makes you happy at the moment you're writing the list, include it. This list has to be 100% honest, or it does you no good. It's not for public consumption, so go ahead and write what's in your heart, and more importantly, allow yourself to be a human being. Forgive yourself if sometimes – hopefully not too often – what makes you happy is not so nice.

The point is, there is no right or wrong way of doing this, as long as you actually do it. Try really hard not to skip a day. One skipped day leads to two skipped days and before long, you've stopped being able to count in your new language because you've forgotten how it's done. It may feel silly at first, or like you are forcing it, but eventually, you'll notice that on some days, you have a hard time keeping yourself to only five, and every once in a while, something so overwhelmingly joyful will happen that you can't wait to write it down so that you'll have it forever.

That brings us to what you do with your Count-to-Five lists. The simple answer is, treat them like any other piece of "homework" you do when learning a new language. If you are someone who always kept your papers for review at the end of the semester, then keep all of your Count-to-Five lists. If you are the type of student who threw a paper away as soon as it was graded, then feel free to toss your list as soon as you make it. Personally, I advise against the latter, because you'll probably enjoy going back and reading your lists from time to time, but if that doesn't suit your personality, don't force it.

Another nice option is to fold every paper in half and keep it in a large jar or shoebox, to be opened and read at the end of the year. Someone suggested to me that the lists be written on index cards and filed chronologically in a recipe box. If that idea works for you, go for it. You'll have a lovely Happiness Almanac that you may wind up keeping for many years.

POP QUIZ!

STOP READING NOW. GRAB a pen and make a list of five things that make you happy. Right now. Do it.

1.

2.

3.

4.

5.

Was that easy? I hope so. If it was easy, you are probably pretty close to being fluent in Happiness.

Or did you skip it and just keep reading? If so, why? Did you have a hard time even coming up with the first one? I can help with that. If you can't come up with even a single thing to put on your Count-to-Five, try this as the first one:

1. I'm happy I can read.

I know it's true, because you are reading this right now. Unless you're listening to this book on tape, in which case, your first number in Happiness is:

1. I'm happy I can hear.

See? You do have things to be happy about. In fact, some of the most basic realities of human nature can make you happy when you just stop to think about them.

Some of my lists include entries like: I'm happy I don't live in a war zone; I'm happy that I have running hot water in my home; I'm happy to have clean sheets on the bed; I'm happy the car started this morning; I'm happy that people don't use outhouses anymore; I'm happy that I've never been truly hungry; I'm happy that I cried for another person today – see, my heart is still open; I'm happy that jackass in the red Toyota got a ticket (Ha!); I'm happy that the cop on the 101 didn't give me a ticket.

There are literally hundreds of things to be happy about each day. Do I remember why the person in the red Toyota was a jackass or deserved a ticket? No. But it makes me happy, even in hindsight, knowing that somehow, in my world that day, justice was done. Do I always want it to be a just world? Clearly not, since not getting a ticket for whatever I was doing on the 101 some other day made me happy as well. That day, justice was not served and that made me perfectly happy.

Here's the thing to remember about your Count-to-Five list – keep it honest. Don't write, "I'm really happy that Christy and I are friends," when what you really want to write is, "Ha-Ha! I am so happy that my blue sweater doesn't look as good on Christy as it does on me!" I mentioned this above with the entry about JoAnn and her boyfriend breaking up. Sometimes, something negative just makes you happy.

It's okay to feel that way. It's even okay to write it down. (It's probably not okay to let Christy or JoAnn know you feel that way, or you might lose a friend.) Although that kind of happiness shouldn't be your primary source of joy in life, don't fight human nature. Allow yourself some guilt-free, nasty happiness every now and then. The Germans even have a word for it: *Schadenfreude* (shod-en-froy-duh) – the joy we get at the misfortune of others. However, try to keep what I call "negative happiness" to a minimum. It'll make you a better person.

And in case you're curious, my Count-to-Five right now, as I type, would be this:

1. I'm happy I'm writing this book. It's really fulfilling and has become a steady source of joy.

2. I'm happy that I thawed out steak for dinner tonight. I love both cooking it and eating it.

3. I'm happy that the air-conditioner is on. It means two things to me – first, that it's comfortable inside as I work, and second, that it's a beautiful sunny day outside.

4. I'm happy that I live in California. I love it here.

5. I'm happy that, at this moment, my husband is dealing with the dog. (It would take too much to explain that, but it makes me SO HAPPY right now.)

Throughout the day, this list changes. Sometimes all five are about how much I love my husband, and sometimes he doesn't make the list at all because so much else is going on. Some days I have really generic entries (I'm happy to be alive; I'm happy to be female; I'm happy to be able to breathe and walk and talk without the aid of machines), and some days it's specific to the point of being weird ("I'm happy that the shoes I returned to Zappos finally got credited back on my Visa bill").

Counting to Five in Happiness can be a signal booster (when you're feeling happy, quickly rattle off a list to make yourself even happier) or a signal disruptor (when you're feeling unhappy, quickly rattle off a list to change your mood), but as you do this more and more, you'll notice that what you write or say doesn't matter, so much as the act of doing it. Which is why you must do it. Like any new language, learning Happiness requires repetition.

CHAPTER

3

Days of the Week and Months of the Year

Sonntag, Montag, Dienstag, Mittwoch, Donnerstag, Freitag, Samstag

Συνδαυ, Μονδαυ, Τυεσδαυ, Ωεδνεσδαυ, Θυρσδαυ, Φριδαυ, Σατυρδαυ

Domenica, Lunedì, Martedì, Mercoledì, Giovedì, Venerdì, Sabato

One of the early lessons in any foreign language is how to say the days of the week and the months of the year.

In Happiness, the days of the week are spoken through daily accomplishments and the months of the year are used to track your natural highs and lows.

How do you get happiness "by the day?" By setting a daily goal you can reach and being happy with yourself for achieving it.

The surest way to be unhappy is to set yourself up for failure. I have been the queen of this in the past. Every day, I would make a to-do list for myself. This list would always include some basic life activities (make chicken for dinner, walk the dog), some admin (pay the electric bill) and at least half a dozen things relating to my work, none of which could all be accomplished within the waking hours of that day. At the end of every day, I would look at the two or three things that didn't get crossed off the list and beat myself up a little over not getting it all done.

Once I started speaking Happiness, I simply changed my approach to the act of making this list, and that changed the outcome. Now, I start each day by looking at what I must do that day or the world will stop turning (walk the dog, pay the electric bill, cook the thawed-out shrimp, etc.), then I look at all of the things I need to get done to sustain my career (return a call to my agent, get through Act II of the latest rewrite), then I look at everything I want to do, either for my career or for myself, that doesn't necessarily *need* to get done today, but has to get done eventually.

Then, I make a much more complete, yet ultimately shorter, list. Because I derive pleasure from crossing things off a list, I design my list for the day so that I can cross everything off with time to spare. I include things that are scheduled (dentist appointment) and things that are a given (shower, eat lunch), not only so that I have more to cross off (Whee!), but also so that I am giving myself credit for time served. You know you have to eat lunch, you know it will take time out of your day (even if you're multitasking while you chew), so put it on the list so that you don't feel like you lost an hour doing "nothing."

My friend David recently taught me a great new technique. When you sit down to write your to-do list, make the first entry, "Prepare a to-do list." That way, the moment you finish, you already get to cross one thing off.

For me, it takes an enormous amount of self-discipline not to keep adding things to the list, especially on days when it doesn't look like anything of value is getting done. However, I realize that my joy in crossing everything off, then discovering I still have an hour left before I need to start dinner (and can throw in a spare activity – something from the "eventually" pile), makes it worth it.

I find that I not only get more done, but that I feel better about myself for doing it. Also, if I get to the point where everything on the list is done and I just don't feel like taking on one more project, I give myself the freedom to goof off for that period of "unscheduled" time, which also puts me in a better mood.

One other reason to make a comprehensive list, besides the fun in crossing off things as you do them, is that it rewards you for how much you really are doing. If you only have two things on a to-do list, and you don't get to one of them, you feel like a lazy bum, even if those two things are: (1) write a novel, and (2) compose a symphony.

However, if your list is…

❊ Walk the dog

❊ Go to the gym

❊ Eat breakfast

❊ Pay bills

❊ Call the insurance company about the car

❊ Reply to email, read industry blogs and newsletters

❊ Work on the novel

❊ Eat lunch

❊ Work some more on the novel

❊ Work on the symphony

❊ Prepare dinner

❊ Do one load of laundry

❊ Watch last night's recorded TV episodes

…then crossing everything off except "Work on the symphony" feels like a lot was done that day. Even better, if you know the chances of getting to the symphony are slim, don't put it on the list. Again, why set yourself up for failure?

Now, if list-making isn't your style, don't force it. No added happiness will come from making a to-do list just for the sake of doing it. However, you still should give yourself a daily dose of accomplishment. For this, think of one thing you need to get done that day (it can be as simple as "Pick up milk on the way home"), then give yourself a little boost of happy when you do it. This may sound wildly trivial to you, but you will be amazed at how happy you can be just by setting one goal each day and achieving it.

You can even set out to make yourself happy by the act of doing your chosen task. In your new language, you say, "Today, I will make myself happy by going to the dentist to get my teeth cleaned. I'm taking care of myself, which makes me feel great and I'll get something unpleasant out of the way for the next six months." At the end of the day, having gone to the dentist, you can reflect on how much happier you are than you were at the start of the day. If you do this once a day, by the end of a month, you will be cumulatively much happier than you were at the beginning of the month. Over the course of a year, there is no limit to how happy your one-a-day accomplishments can make you.

Other examples of how to start your day:

❃ "Today I'll make myself happy by finishing the marketing report. It's due today, so I'll be successful in my job by completing it, and I'll have the joy of a job well done."

❊ "Today I'll make myself happy by not letting Andrew's snide comments bother me. Whenever he starts criticizing my work, I will just remind myself that he is not my boss, I'm very good at what I do, and his feedback is in a language I don't have to speak anymore."

❊ "Today I'll make myself happy by reading to the kids before they go to bed. I often run out of time for that, but this one day, I will make it my top priority. I love spending that time with them and I'm not going to sacrifice it just to get the dishes done or the laundry folded. Those things can wait."

❊ "Today I'll make myself happy by kissing my wife as soon as she walks in the door. Sometimes I forget, but today, I will make it the one thing I am sure to do."

Learning the days of the week in Happiness is one of those skills that requires repetition, but soon becomes second nature. Each day is a new chance to practice.

Learning the months of the year in Happiness serves a different purpose. I learned this lesson when my husband and I were trying to conceive and I had to keep a fertility diary. An interesting pattern emerged. The days when I seemed to be really nasty, or short-tempered, were always either Day 21 or Day 22 of my cycle. Although no woman ever wants to admit that she's got PMS, and even though I didn't have a single other symptom, it couldn't go unnoticed that I just wasn't very nice to him during that time.

There is real freedom in this discovery. To clarify, knowing the root cause hasn't given me the freedom to be a raging shrew, it's given us the freedom to adjust, and even laugh about it. Now that I know my calendar in Happiness, when I get snippy, or nasty, or just feel in a foul mood, I can look at what day it is and say, "Okay, this is not me. I am not this horrible person. In less than 48 hours, I will be back to my regular, happy self." I've even given my husband permission to remind me (gently) what day it is, in case he's bearing the brunt of it.

The Happiness calendar is not reserved to women. Do you keep a daily, weekly or monthly calendar for work, social or health reasons? If so, find a way to notate every time you are in an unusually crappy mood. After three months, see if there is a pattern.

When I first thought of including this concept in the book, I asked several friends, both men and women, if they'd ever noticed patterns like this. All of the women mentioned at some point becoming aware of foul moods coinciding with their monthly cycles, but interestingly enough, two of the men had patterns of their own.

One man noticed that he got very short-tempered every other Thursday. (Okay, the truth is, his wife noticed, but at least he acknowledged it.) It turns out, that was the day before his commission check came in and he was very tense about it. There were numerous issues surrounding the check that were out of his control (like not getting his commission when clients hadn't paid their bills yet, or having larger-than-expected expenses deducted), and the uncertainty made him crazy. We talked about what he did to combat this, and make him nicer to his wife and kids on those days, and he told me he joined a Thursday-night bowling league. That cracked me up. Perhaps the simplest of all solutions (distance), but it worked for all concerned.

Another man noticed that his unpleasantness seemed to coincide with his girlfriend's cycle. He finally made the connection that they only fought three days of the month, and even after he discovered it, she wasn't willing to concede that it was hormonal. No problem. Once he was aware of the pattern, he was able to adjust, and maintain his own happiness without letting the conflict escalate. Even though she still has her PMS moments, they are both happier because the conflict is less and nobody's behavior is leading to lingering, long-term resentments.

Why fight Mother Nature? If you are on any kind of a cycle that brings you regular unhappiness, spot it, fix it (as much as you can), and don't slide backwards into your native language. You've learned how to say the days and months in Happiness. Now, practice perfecting them.

CHAPTER

4

THE USE OF COLORS IN THE LANGUAGE OF HAPPINESS

rouge, orange, jaune, vert, bleu, indigo, violet

、赤い、オレンジ、黄色い、緑のすみれ色インディゴ青い

красно, померанцово, желто, зелено, голубо, индиго, лиловое

Okay, I know it's cheesy to use the colors of the rainbow to open any conversation about being happy, so let's ditch all seven of them and concentrate on just one color.

Pick a color right now that you think of as happy.

No, seriously. If I say, "That's a happy color," what color did you think of? In this chapter, you will learn how to use that color to trigger happiness.

As it turns out, color can be a great mood changer. In preparing to write this book, I studied several language textbooks. In all of them, there was a section fairly early on about learning the colors in your new language, which I breezed past, thinking colors had nothing to do with speaking Happiness. Then, one day while reading a Spanish book, I discovered the following practice sentence: "El color azul siempre me hace sentir feliz." ("The color blue always makes me feel happy.")

Wow. The more I thought about it, the more I realized it was right. The color blue does always make me feel happy. In fact, I was so impressed by this idea, that I shared it with some friends at a dinner party to see if they agreed, and if there was a way to turn that into a happiness exercise. The flaw in my approach was that I insisted we all use the color blue, so even though the experiment worked, it would have worked much better if each person had chosen the color for themselves that truly engendered happiness, which is what you will do to make this work for you. More on that later.

At the dinner party, sticking with "el color azul," I shared the fact that since I moved to California, I have discovered a new color in the spectrum. I call it California Blue Sky. I don't know why this is true, but on a clear day, the sky out here is a shade of deep periwinkle that I have never seen anywhere else on the planet, and no matter what else is going on in my day, if I can stop and look at the sky and see that color, it makes me happy.

I asked my friends how the color blue makes them happy. It took a while to get warmed up, but pretty soon we were six-for-six (including my blue-sky story) for everyone having a way that a color (in this case, blue) made them happy. Here are their replies:

1. "When I was a kid, we weren't allowed to use real drinking glasses except at dinner. There were six of us, and my mom just knew we would break one every day if we had the chance, so she had these stupid blue tumblers and they were the only thing we could drink out of. I HATED them. But now, every time I'm in a place like Target or Bed, Bath & Beyond and I see cups like that, or any plastic crap that color, it makes me smile."

2. "My nephew's baby blanket was blue. That was the coolest thing ever. Going home at spring break and holding him for the first time."

3. "Dude, my Mustang." (This elicited a big "Well, duh!" from the rest of us. When someone has a '68 Mustang in the original Acapulco Blue, it's almost redundant to ask if the color blue makes him happy.)

4. "I was on a cruise once with my family and one night after dinner I walked around the whole boat by myself, and I finally understood what the color Navy Blue really is. You could tell it wasn't black, you know? But it was so dark, and almost mesmerizing."

Our last guest couldn't come up with anything. I wasn't prepared to go five-for-six, so we started asking him about any memories of blue, happy or not. Finally, he remembered a girl he went to college with who had super-blue eyes. As he described it, her eyes were the kind of color that people now assume is fake because it's that unnaturally beautiful. He was obsessed with her. He wound up driving her home from a party one night, and they talked until the wee hours, but it turned out she had a boyfriend at another school, so it went nowhere. The thing we all noticed was the giant smile he had on his face and...well, almost a blush in his cheeks as he talked about her. Finally, I had to point out that he seemed really to be happy as he relayed the story, to which he replied, "Yeah. That was a pretty special night."

That's when I decided to turn our dinner game into an experiment. I asked everyone at the table to spend the next week letting the color blue make them happy.

The idea was that every time they saw the color blue, they should let it trigger the happy thought that they shared that night, whether it was a memory of holding a baby or looking deep into the blue eyes of an unobtainable co-ed. Could happiness be sustained, or at least given a boost, by associating it with a color?

As it turns out, the answer is yes. Everyone had the same experience – by the end of the week, they'd all had several moments of seeing the color blue and being reminded to be happy.

Look around you right now. How many places do you spot the color blue? Or red? Or burgundy? What if every time you noticed something that color it made you happy, or at least gave you a temporary flash to a happy memory? If you start actively associating a color with happiness, it won't be long before the simple sight of that color triggers a happy reaction in your brain.

As stated above, it doesn't have to be blue. Did your high school sweetheart's house have an awesome red door that made you a little giddy every time you knocked on it? Does your favorite sports team wear green jerseys? Does someone in your life leave you yellow post-it notes that brighten your day? Did you have a favorite black shirt that made you look really sexy? Think hard, and try not to fake this one – somewhere in your life, there is a color you can associate with absolute happiness, and even thinking about it now makes you smile. Got it? Have you figured out your color?

Look around you. How many places do you see that color? Kind of surprising, isn't it? Do you see it more than you would have thought? I hope so. Now, make a concerted effort to mentally mark each of those red or green or purple spots and let them remind you how happy that color makes you. For the next week, notice your color everywhere you go. It is yours now – you own it, and you can use it to trigger that joyful thought and ultimately make yourself really happy.

CHAPTER

5

VERBS – PART ONE

I celebrate.
You laugh.
She smiles.
They dance.
We love.

Every new language requires the student to learn the basic verbs and how to conjugate them – what form the verb takes when talking about oneself (I), one's partner (you), others (he/she/they), or all of us together (we). In the language of Happiness, the only form of the verb that matters is the "I" form.

Why? Because your actions – your Happiness verbs – cannot make others happy, and you cannot depend on the "verbs" (i.e., actions) of others to make you happy, nor to allow them to make you unhappy.

The four key verbs of Happiness are respect, release, remember and reward. If you can master all four of these, you will achieve a solid basis in your new language. You'll notice that some of the obvious ones (love, laugh, celebrate, etc.) are missing from this list. The reason is that those are situational verbs.

A situational verb requires you to be in a particular place, time or condition. To love – actively, as a verb – you need an object of love: something or someone to actually love. Laughing and celebrating are wonderful and joyous, but you can get through a day where you found nothing particularly funny to laugh at or specifically joyous to celebrate and still be happy. This chapter and the next are devoted to those verbs you can perform on your own, without the aid or hindrance of others, and which, over time, will make you a happy person.

Respect

This is the most fundamental verb in the language of happiness, because if you do not actively respect yourself and others, you will have a void that is filled with verbs like criticize, undermine, judge, regret or even just ignore – all actions that contribute to unhappiness.

Your mother probably told you that if you date someone who is nice to you, but mean to the waitress, break it off, because that is not a good person. (Unless your mother was the one being mean to the waitress, which indicates that Happiness was clearly not her native language.) Eliminating the concept of someone being a "good" or "bad" person, anyone who is mean to the waitress/gardener/cashier is not happy, and you need to consider how much unhappiness like that you want in your life. I have never known a truly happy person who was regularly mean to others, especially those in less fortunate circumstances.

Happy people do not feel the need to belittle anyone. Happy people do not make themselves larger by making other people smaller, and they don't take joy in making other people unhappy. If you aim to eventually be fluent in Happiness, you are going to have to spend as much time as you can with those who already speak this language, or, like you, are learning it. This means spotting the people who are incapable of Happiness and limiting your exposure to them.

If you are unable to do that, recognize that they can be a negative influence and do what you can to minimize that influence. If you have to be around people who treat others with disrespect, don't emulate them. It's hard to respect yourself when you don't respect anyone else, and it is nearly impossible to be happy if you don't respect yourself.

Also, actively respecting others makes you feel *great!* No, you should not give yourself a huge pat on the back because you weren't rude to the bus driver - that's the baseline. What you will notice is that every time you could have chosen anger, disrespect, criticism or old-fashioned nastiness, but instead chose humanity and dignity, you walked away feeling like a better person, and that eventually leads to the most important verb of Happiness – Respect – as you apply it to yourself.

If you do not currently respect yourself (actively – in verb form), then this is going to be the hardest work you do in this entire book. You will want to mark this chapter and come back to it often, as a reminder of the place you need to be in order to be fluent in your new language.

The first step is to always actively respect others. This is not simply about the checker at the grocery store, but also your mother, your teenager, the neighbor whose trash cans always block your driveway. It's a challenging thing to do, and I deliberately chose examples of people you may feel don't always deserve your respect (since they are not respecting you), but you have to remember – this is about you, not them. The more you respect others, the more you can develop a solid ability to respect yourself. With this newfound skill, you will also be able to extract yourself from situations that may cause you to stop respecting yourself.

How many times have you walked away from dealing with someone and just hated yourself for the way you behaved, or worse, what they were able to get from you? I have a former friend who cannot say, "No." Need someone to help you move? Drive you to the airport? Donate a kidney? She's there. And sadly, many people in her life take advantage of this.

That would be fine if she simply loved the act of helping, but often she feels burdened by the requests, even as she's carrying them out. I repeatedly tried to show her that the world doesn't end when you say no to someone (I say no all the time), and any friendship that requires this sort of one-sided devotion is not worth maintaining, but when she was growing up, the primary language spoken to her by her mother was Disrespect, so it became her native language.

As much as I wanted to help her find respect for herself, I realized after several years of trying that this was futile, and slowly allowed the friendship to dissolve, not only because her overwrought laments about what her friends were "making" her do were growing tiresome, but also because I noticed that when we went out together, she was almost always unkind to the waitress.

With that example, we come full circle to the idea that you cannot be happy until you respect yourself, and you won't achieve true respect for yourself until you can actively respect others – even those who you feel haven't "earned" it.

With your parent or your child, are you listening to what they're saying – actually hearing their opinions or concerns? If you were in their position, how would you expect to be treated? What can you do to respect that person? Sometimes, listening is all it takes. The magic of this is that over time, they are likely to start actively showing their respect in return by listening to you.

When I say over time, I mean months, even years... not days. You also have to limit your expectations of someone else's respect for you to their capabilities.

Do you get mad at your dog because he can't drive your car? No? Then why get mad at your teenager because he doesn't know how to show respect for your years of wisdom? Were you able to do that at his age?

It was not until I left school and started practicing law that I finally began respecting what my mother did for us. In my mind, I knew that she worked long hours and was the sole supporter of my sister and me, but it never really registered what that meant until I got my first real job, and had a mortgage, and was the sole supporter of my family (consisting of me and a rescue-dog named Jasmine).

Lord, was that HARD! How does anyone do it as a single mom with two kids and a lot less money? Sheesh!

However, at 14, respecting her was not in my skill set. Just as respecting me was not in hers. Her childhood had been incredibly rough compared to mine. She looked at my fourteen-year-old existence as one long trip to the amusement park, and as much as she loved me, rather than respect herself for all that she had been able to give to me by sheer force of her own strength of character, she resented how easy I had it, comparatively.

I spent most of my teen years being told that I didn't have real problems and didn't know what real problems were, which sadly resulted in me never talking to my mom about whatever was going on in my life. I can't hold that against her, however. This woman single-handedly moved mountains, and very rarely was she ever shown the respect she deserved, particularly by her mother and siblings. It is one of her greatest sources of unhappiness, and one of the reasons I chose Respect as the most important verb in Happiness.

How do you get to a point where you actively respect yourself, if you have not been offered respect for most of your life? Look at the people you most respect in the world, figure out why you respect them, then behave in the way you regard as respectable, thus recognizing yourself as deserving of respect.

This is why in Happiness, respect is a verb, not a noun. It is an action, and it requires constant exercise to stay fit.

Some examples of my own work in this area:

1. I respected my grandmother's ability to keep everyone's confidences. Anyone could tell her anything with the certainty that it would never be revealed. In my life, particularly in my youth, this was a struggle for me. I was a natural

blabbermouth, which got me in a lot of trouble and ended more than one friendship. So now, whenever I am faced with the choice between telling a secret or not, I think about Grammy, and how much I respected that trait in her, and I do the thing that I find respectable. The result – I actively respect myself. More importantly, I don't fall back into old habits (i.e., gossip) that cause me to lose respect for myself.

2. I am brought to tears every time I see the picture of the young man in Tiananmen Square standing in front of a battalion of tanks. For a long time, primarily because I work in the film industry, I smiled and nodded at whatever offensive thing was being said, never speaking out for fear that it might cost me an opportunity. But when I thought of what that young man sacrificed for his beliefs, I realized that I could no longer allow myself to sit by and tolerate behavior and attitudes that I abhor simply on the chance that someone might throw a little work my way. Finally, one day, I decided that it was better to do the right thing than to get the job.

I was meeting with an executive whose company had decided to make only "urban films," which in Hollywood is code for material aimed at African-Americans. As her explanation of the company's view of this audience and their tastes got increasingly offensive, I got increasingly uncomfortable, and when she started a sentence with, "Those people..." I stopped her, explained why I would never work for her or that company, and walked out.

No, it's not standing in front of a tank, but I did the thing that I would find respectable, and for Happiness, that is all that's required. On a side note – that company went under within a year of that meeting.

3. My mother and my sister both became single mothers, after more than a decade of marriage each, with limited resumés and two children to support. Instead of sitting around feeling sorry for themselves, they both worked tirelessly to find jobs which would pay enough to care for their families and at which they could succeed and grow. My mom is now happily retired with a very healthy nest egg, and my sister is a highly respected professional in her field.

After watching them re-invent themselves, I knew that when the winds changed in my own industry (after a prolonged strike, during which I committed the cardinal sin of turning 40 – an almost mandatory retirement age for screenwriters), I could do nothing less than find a way to use the talents I possess in a whole new field. Writing this book makes me happy, because doing so gives me the chance to emulate two women I truly respect, and thus gain respect for myself.

The main thing to remember is that being happy is a state, not an action. It is what you are (as you learned in Chapter One – "I am happy"), but it results from actively doing things that will make you happy, such as respecting yourself and others. The next chapter will explain the other three action verbs in Happiness – Remember, Release and Reward. When you are adept at these four, you can count on your happiness becoming as native to you as the language you naturally speak.

CHAPTER

6

VERBS – PART TWO

Remember, Release and Reward

I n the last chapter, we talked about how important it is to regard the verb Respect as an action. Yes, you may be sitting motionless while performing it, but you have to realize that when you respect yourself and others, you are actively doing something to make yourself happy.

In this chapter, we'll look at three other actions that foster happiness – Remember, Release and Reward.

Remember

As you've read in previous chapters, I am a to-do list maker. This is not for everyone, but it works for me, except when it makes me feel awful about myself.

One day a few months back, as it was approaching 6:00 p.m., I looked at my list and there was not one thing I could cross off. It was due to a combination of distractions, email, changing priorities, and probably a dose of just plain laziness, but basically, nothing was getting done.

And what does a girl of the millennium do when she is mad at herself for not getting anything done? Clearly, she goes on Facebook to tell her 400 friends that she is not getting anything done. I'm not sure if this was public self-flagellation or an attempt to garner sympathy (and exoneration), but that day, I posted as my status update: "I wish I was getting more accomplished today."

Almost instantly, my incredibly witty cousin, Heidi, replied, "I don't know - I think you're pretty accomplished already."

Aside from being a wonderful play on words, Heidi's note gave me a moment to pause and actively remember what would cause her to say that about me. At the time, I was going through some serious career difficulties, and was feeling like a real failure. Stopping to remember what I achieved in the past, even in the absence of such achievements at the time, was a great boost to my happiness.

In a later chapter we are going to talk about the dangers of relying on past happiness too much, but for now, stop and actively remember at least three things you've done (actions you've taken – not something anyone else did for you) that made you happy.

Are you struggling with this? If so, it may be that you are discounting your past happy-making actions, either because you think they aren't important enough or because you feel egotistical including them. Erase those judgments from your mind.

Here's the rule to follow: Did you do it? Did it make you happy? Then actively Remember it.

Want some examples? Here are some of the very small, but lovely ones that I rotate through now and then.

1. In fourth grade, I was the first girl to learn how to French braid hair, and I was able to do all the other girls' hair during recess. This made me very popular.

2. At a football game in high school, my boyfriend, Jeff, and his friend Paul would not stop talking about the pizza that was in Paul's car that they had bought for themselves (and themselves only) for after the game. My friend Michelle and I stole it. It tasted great. Paul spent years trying to figure out who took his pizza that night, until I finally told him it was us. He's still mad. I am laughing just thinking about this. (Paul laughs about it now, too, and I have since bought him many a pizza.)

3. The men's and women's soccer teams at Trinity University came back to campus two weeks early

for pre-season practice, so we had the school to ourselves, which was awesome. One night, I ran into a friend from the men's team and he revealed that he had fallen in love for the first time that summer. We walked back to campus and he could not stop talking about it, so we climbed onto the roof of the study hall next to my dorm and talked until the sun came up. We got our butts kicked at practice that day, but I didn't care. That is still one of the most wonderful nights of my life.

4. An old woman showed up at my doorstep in LA one day, lost and disoriented. She was in my neighborhood because her sister lived nearby. I got my keys, and she and I got into my car and we drove around in the hopes that she would recognize the place. She didn't, but she knew the name of her sister's synagogue. I took her there and the rabbi called her sister to come get her. She tried to pay me, but there was no way I was taking her money. She turned to the rabbi and said something in Yiddish, then turned and told me that she was telling him I was an angel. That memory fills me with extreme joy.

5. Saving the very smallest act for last – I actively remember the day I finally stormed out of the front door of my house in Oakland, garden shears in hand, and cut down the top of the bougainvillea climbing up the outside wall of my house and

blocking my beautiful view. I felt a thousand pounds of anger towards that plant dissipate in moments, and every time I walked through my dining room and glanced out the window, I was filled with happiness about what I had done.

Yes, there are far more momentous, significant, happiness-inspiring acts in my past – graduations, starting (and quitting) jobs, getting married, selling screenplays, but so what? The tiny things listed above are things that I did, and they made me happy, and just thinking about them now makes me happy all over again. That's the point of actively seeing happiness when you cause it for yourself, and savoring it. So that when you are trying to speak Happiness, you'll easily Remember.

Release

When you master the act (and art) of Release, you will be well on your way to being fluent in Happiness. One of the most important steps in being happy is ridding yourself of the things that make you unhappy. Whether it's beating yourself up over an incident that didn't turn out as you would have liked, or holding a grudge against someone who wronged you, or blaming the universe when things don't turn out your way, the negative weight of past unhappiness can really inhibit your ability to be truly happy now.

Release as a verb is distinct from "forgive." I find forgiveness to be a much greater challenge, and as applies to what you want – happiness – forgiving is not required.

Let me make the distinction clear, so you can begin the act of releasing. Imagine something horrible happening to you or a loved one at the hands of another person. Everyone has their own sensibilities, so think of what, for you, would cause the most unimaginable heartbreak. Now, think about what it would take to forgive the person who committed that act.

I don't know about you, but I am simply not capable of that level of forgiveness. I am not Jesus, Gandhi, Buddha, Martin Luther King, Jr., the Dalai Lama or any other great spirit who can achieve that kind of transcendence.

I am an average woman, born on the East Coast, raised in the Midwest, matriculated in Texas and now living in Los Angeles, and I can't even forgive the duplicitous jerk who betrayed my husband in a business deal four years ago, much less someone who would do serious harm to my family. But I can be happy, even in a world where those people exist, because I can Release my hatred for them. I can take a moment and feel it leaving my body.

I don't forgive the people who have hurt the ones I love – they are not absolved. However, their past or current behavior does not have to control me, or my emotions. You don't have to forgive to stop being angry, you just have to release.

And much like the act of Remembering, releasing can be tiny. Don't just Release the overwhelming emotions from being victimized or deeply harmed, but every wrong done to you, either by others or by you, yourself. When you feel the buildup of resentment, anger, frustration or whatever clouds your happiness, target where it's coming from and simply release it. Releasing is a physical act. Stop and feel it happening.

Is the person in front of you at the drive-through taking far longer than he should when you're already twenty-two minutes late to pick up your daughter? How does it feel, sitting here getting angry at him, or at yourself for being in this situation? Make a quick decision about whether you can change your circumstances and if you can't, sit back and Release.

This realization of our need to release things in this way came to me one day at the dog park. Actually, it was screamed in my vicinity. A woman was trying to get a toy away from her dog, and with her holding one end and the dog firmly gripping the other between his teeth, she was shrieking at him, "*Release! Release! Release!*" I watched as her sheer rage built, and it occurred to me that any vestige of happiness she might have gotten from bringing her dog to the park was long gone, and no matter what else happened, she was not going to get it back.

She had so much invested in getting the dog to give her the toy, but what if she had just let it go, actively

Released her own need to be...I don't know...obeyed? Respected? Dominant? Would the outcome have been different? She still would not have gotten the toy, but she would have been happier, or at least more able to respect herself.

When the shrieking got to be too much (and our pity for the poor dog reached its peak), a dog park regular who is always equipped in such situations trotted over and asked if he could give the stubborn animal a treat. As soon as the liver nuggets appeared, the dog instantly dropped the toy and the woman snatched it up. Even if that moment gave her a small rush of victory (she wound up with the toy, after all), I can't imagine that she felt all that happy. How could she?

Try this – when you feel yourself getting agitated, depressed or even resigned to failure, stop and ask if there is something you can Release that will leave you feeling closer to happy. Release the judgment you pass on yourself for being in this situation. Release the anger you are aiming at the person you think is responsible for your negative mood. Release the grudge you are holding against anyone whose past behavior might have caused your current reality. Release begrudging the victor, simply because it is not you.

You don't have to forgive. You don't have to forget. You simply have to lean back and feel the unhappiness leaving your body as you Release.

Reward

Do something nice for yourself. It's that simple. Reward yourself for...well...whatever you choose to reward yourself for. Pick a goal, and once you achieve it, give yourself a pre-determined reward. Or, on the other hand, if you are walking down the street and you actively Respect someone who you encounter, you Remember a small moment of happiness, or you Release a negative attitude that could have stopped you from being happy, acknowledge how far you've come in learning this new language and Reward yourself for that.

Rewards can come in all shapes and sizes. They can be extravagant expenditures that you've been saving up for, or they can be tiny compliments that you give yourself for a job well done. Or even just for being you.

I realize this makes me sound crazy, but in my to-do list world, I reward myself for completing everything on the day's list by making the list for the next day before calling it quits for the night. Making the list is an act I truly enjoy, it's something I need to do anyway, and when I think of it as an act of rewarding myself, I feel a little extra joy.

When you feel happy, Reward yourself for achieving that state of mind, and while you're at it, Reward the people around you.

Do you have any idea how easy, cheap and thrilling it is to give someone a nice compliment? You are rewarding them while at the same time rewarding yourself for having the generosity of spirit to make another person feel good, even if you feel crappy yourself right now.

If there is anyone else in your vicinity at this moment, stop, put down the book, and think about something genuinely kind that you can say. Do it! Even if it's a total stranger. Does she have pretty shoes? Is he doing something daring or interesting? You are a smart enough person to come up with something to say that will make both you and the other person happier. The other day, going into a Walgreens, I passed a woman wearing a long, summer dress, and as I walked by, I pointed to her outfit and said, "That is so lovely," and I kept going. I heard her stunned, "Thank you," as I entered the store, but I didn't need that. I didn't say it for her benefit, I said it for mine. The nice thing is, it really was for both of us.

And what if the person in your vicinity is the nasty woman in the next cubicle who makes everyone's life in the office miserable? (This is the person my mother refers to as the Stapler Nazi, and for some inexplicable reason, every office has one.) Don't force yourself. If it is not going to make you feel good saying it, it's not a reward, for you or them.

I used to discuss this point by saying, "Everyone loves to get gifts," until a relative said to me, "You don't." That knocked me back a step, but the truth is, I am not a good gift recipient. It is something I have to work on.

Somewhere in my past, maybe I got the notion that I wasn't deserving of gifts, or that no one would ever know me well enough to get the right thing, but I got a lucky push in the right direction recently when my Aunt Jane wanted to give me something that I refused, thinking it was too lavish and really not necessary, and she replied, "Who are you to tell me what I can and can't give to you as a gift? I wouldn't be giving it if I didn't want to. Besides, it gives me joy to give things to you and you don't have the right to take that away from me."

There is so much wisdom in this that I can't even begin to express the difference it's made. If you will get joy from the act of giving someone a gift, give it. If someone will get joy from giving you a gift, receive it.

One of the greatest lessons I ever learned was about ten years ago, from a young, African-American girl at McDonald's. I was standing in line and I glanced over and noticed her in the next line. She was maybe eight years old and had the most perfect features I have ever seen on a living person. She literally looked like a painting, and without realizing it, I just looked at her and said, "You are absolutely beautiful."

Her face registered a moment of delighted surprise, then she broke into a huge smile and said, "Thank you."

That was it. Our entire conversation. Unlike me, she didn't have the need to say, "No, I've gained a lot of weight," or "But you should see me when I don't have make-up on." She received my compliment openly (something I did not yet do), and with her happiness, Rewarded me.

Remember what you do to make yourself happy.

Release the negativity that blocks your happiness.

Reward yourself and others when you are happy.

And ALWAYS

Respect yourself and those around you.

Respect, remember, release and reward. Conjugate to your heart's delight. You are almost completely conversational in Happiness and very close to being fluent. Someday, you may even pass yourself off as a native speaker.

CHAPTER

7

NOUNS

In second grade, you learned that a noun is a person, place or thing. In the language of Happiness, nouns are much simpler than that.

A person or a place may make you happy, for a time at least, but as we'll discuss in Chapter Ten, that's situational happiness. Therefore, nouns in Happiness don't include persons or places, only "things."

To achieve permanent happiness, you have to embrace two key nouns as if they were actual, physical objects you can hold in your hand, and reject one important one, the existence of which does more to destroy happiness than any other "person, place or thing" in your life today.

The nouns of Happiness – the things you need to be able to create and hold - are Motion and Satisfaction, and the thing you must toss out is Fear.

Motion. noun.

1. MOVEMENT – progress, passage, transit, shift, travel

2. GESTURE – signal, sign, indication

Motion, as defined in Happiness, is that thing which takes you from Point A to Point B.   Are you happy right now? No? Then you need Motion. It's that simple.

It is not possible to be happy if you're stagnant. It's especially not possible if you start at unhappy, but even once you get to the point of being happy, you cannot just stop and look around and say, "Okay, everyone and everything else freeze! I'm happy. Don't change a thing." Life just doesn't work that way.

The two possible meanings of Motion in our new language are Movement and Gesture. Both are required for happiness. Movement is transition. It is getting from the status quo to the place you want to be (or at least closer). It can be progress or it can take you backwards, but here's one thing you know for sure – without movement, progress is impossible.

A motion is also a gesture – some sign for you to heed or look out for. An indication that you are now speaking a new language. The signal that in this situation, you could easily have reverted to your native language and gotten angry or mean, but you instead chose to speak Happiness, actively respecting and releasing in a way that may not have given anyone else involved satisfaction (as we'll discuss below), but will leave you feeling better – happier.

How do you harness Motion, and bring it into your daily vocabulary? It's this simple – don't stay still. Each day, do one act that is motivated by your happiness. You don't have to plan for this, you may just reflect on it at the end of the day and realize it happened, or it may be a decision you make at the spur of the moment, but once you launch into motion, you will be amazed at how easily you can stay in motion. What this means is that once happiness is your motivator, it is far easier to maintain.

Some words of caution – there is a difference between being motivated by your own happiness and being selfish. Your happiness should not come at someone else's expense, but don't forget that theirs should not come at your expense either. Let me try to give an example that may make this clear.

I have a friend who has two fairly willful children. Often she feels that it's her against them (a not-so-healthy parent-child dynamic) and that she has given up all of the things she loves to put them first. One of those things is gourmet cooking. While grocery shopping one day (with them in tow), she splurged and bought a rack of lamb to cook for dinner that night. The idea of it just tickled her fancy at that moment, and she told me she was almost giddy at the thought of making roasted rack of lamb for the first time in ages. Unfortunately, on the way home, the girls started saying they wanted McDonald's for dinner.

Now, usually this wouldn't be much of a fight, because the girls saying they wanted it meant that they got it, but this night, she really wanted to cook that rack of lamb. After numerous conversations with me about how to include her happiness in the equation, and that occasionally their immediate happiness would have to be sacrificed so that she could be happy, too, she decided this time to try a little Motion. She pulled over, turned to face the girls, and with total respect said, "No. We are not going to McDonald's. We are going home and I'm cooking the lamb."

When later recounting this, she told me she could barely wipe the smile off her face for the rest of the drive home, even as their wails turned into tears. She was overwhelmed by the joy of having made a decision based on her own happiness, and at that moment, knew that she had turned a corner.

The girls continued to protest, and one of them even refused to eat anything other than McDonald's that night (boy, was she surprised when Mommy told her that if she got hungry, a plate of lamb would be waiting). However, this was the first step in an incredible journey that has led to so much more respect and reward than any of the three of them could have imagined.

It turns out, not getting their way that night not only didn't kill her children, it made them realize that what their mother wanted was important, too. That's a significant first step for them, as it will make it easier for them to actively respect other people (and themselves) later in life, which as we know, is a requirement for their true happiness.

If you cannot relate at all to this story, because you don't have children or because your children happen to be perfect, think about whose happiness you are basing your decisions on, if not your own. Is it a parent? Your best friend? Your spouse? Some pushy neighbor? Try this next time you are put in a position where your happiness will be lessened to increase theirs – say, "No." It will require boundless courage, and you will have to actively Release any guilt it might cause (especially as they work to make you feel guiltier), but you may be surprised to find that the world does not stop turning.

It's hard to make your happiness a priority, but if you try to explain it in simple terms, with respect, then hold your ground, you will discover that it's incredibly empowering. Almost supernaturally so.

Of course, I am not advocating unmitigated selfishness, and one of the reasons we do things that we don't enjoy to benefit others is that it will give us greater happiness in the long run. However, if you find that any relationship is always about the other person's happiness and rarely, if ever, about yours, you need to end (or adjust the terms of) that relationship. You have the tricky task now of determining when your happiness depends on exercising a little selfishness, and where to draw the line. This may be very tough, but it all starts with a little happiness-motivated Motion.

Satisfaction. noun.

1. CONTENTMENT – pleasure, fulfillment, enjoyment, gratification

2. COMPENSATION (like the satisfaction of a debt) – payment, redress, settlement

If you allow yourself to accept it, the result of Motion is Satisfaction. Remember my friend with her daughters? She launched a huge Motion by saying no to them, but it would have had no effect on her happiness, except maybe a negative one, if she had spent the rest of the night second-guessing her movement and changing her mind and beating herself up for it.

To be fluent in Happiness, you have to hold in your hand the contentment you will get from making decisions based on your happiness. It is your reward – your payment – for having the courage not to stay still.

There is a person in my life who has the worst case of buyer's remorse I have ever witnessed. Worse – she's a terrible impulse shopper, including things like cars and houses (and no, she's not wealthy by any stretch; she just manages her money very well – something she should Reward herself for more often). It doesn't matter what she's purchased, she beats herself up over it endlessly, until ultimately she decides to keep whatever she's bought (with some regret), decides to return it (with some regret), or finds that she cannot return it (which leads to regret, panic over whether she should have ever bought it, and a bit of self-loathing for having it – even something she loved when purchased). It's terribly sad.

This regretful buyer has flashes of Motion, when she buys something she wants and can perfectly afford, but she can't follow that with Satisfaction. Her happiness is not enough of a motivator, and I can say with some authority (this is someone I am *very* close to), it's because she has never actively Respected herself enough to understand how much she deserves these rewards. An even sadder reality is that she has absolutely no problem spending her money on other people. No remorse, no regret, even when they prove unworthy of her generosity.

Does any part of that pattern sound familiar to you? How much do you punish yourself for splurging on you? Do you go into a moral frenzy for saying no to someone else? If that's not you, then wonderful! You already know how to use the noun Satisfaction when speaking

Happiness. But if it is you, stop and ask yourself why. If you can't figure it out, go back to the verbs and make sure you are actively performing all of them on a daily basis.

Also, I don't want anyone to think that Motion and Satisfaction are only about buying things for yourself or saying no to people.

Today, I had go to a store to return several items that I had bought for full price but found on sale somewhere else. This is the kind of task I hate, and it makes me do everything that is the opposite of Respecting and Rewarding myself.

I hate that I bought something too soon when if I'd just waited it would have gone on sale (how stupid a thought is this? I don't have a crystal ball!). I hate that I can't live my life as if money were no object (which is something I would never do anyway!). I hate that I spent an hour doing something that only saved me $43 (because I want to tell myself that my time is worth so much more than $43 an hour).

Then, on the way home, while stewing, I drove past a little girl and her father, on the corner of Sycamore Avenue and Third Street, selling lemonade. Yep, a real honest-to-goodness lemonade stand. At that moment, I made a quick choice to employ a little Motion to change my foul mood.

I made the next right, circled the block and went back to that corner. As I pulled to a stop and rolled down the window, the little girl's face lit up like fireworks. I called out the window, "How much?" and the dad answered, "Fifty cents a cup!" So I said, "I'll take one, please." I can't quite describe the joy on this child's face as she poured my lemonade, brought it to my car, took my change and ran back to her dad. I took a sip (it was awful) and said, "It's delicious!" The dad said, "Thank you," in that tone that made me realize they had been there in the heat for a while with not a lot of business, and I probably made his daughter's day, which in turn made his. That gave me a whole boatload of Satisfaction, which carried me all the way home and into the night, wiping out all the exasperation that preceded it.

❄❄❄

A Happiness Noun Exercise

Today, perform a Motion motivated strictly by your own happiness, then take Satisfaction from having done it. Afterwards, give yourself a reminder of what you did (a post-it note that you can look at throughout the day; a little star drawn on your wrist; anything). Every time you look at your reminder, actively Remember your Motion and embrace your Satisfaction all over again. In short – be happy.

Fear. noun.

1. ALARM – panic, agitation, dread, distress, unease, foreboding, trepidation, aversion, anxiety, neurosis

Fear is the one noun that can utterly destroy your happiness. I am not talking about the verb "to fear" – the act of sensing danger and triggering your fight or flight instinct. I am talking about the basic fear that weighs on your brain like a stone every time you consider a Motion motivated by your happiness.

"Will it make people mad?" "What if I can't undo it?" "What will my family think?" "This might subject me to ridicule." "I will die if people laugh at me."

The Fear you cling to is strangling your happiness. Imagine yourself physically taking it out of your brain and putting it in a box. You can go visit it now and then, but please don't take it out and try it back on.

I have to share a story about Fear that may surprise you, or make you say, "If I had all that, there's no way I'd be unhappy!" However, think about all that you do have, and what you are keeping yourself from enjoying by holding onto your Fear.

One of my dearest friends is a successful accountant who was married to another successful accountant for 17 years, until her husband decided that his firm's 25-year-old event planner was "more fun" than she was and moved in with her. She came away from the divorce with a condo in San Francisco and a hefty monthly alimony payment.

Staying in her home in the city, she continued to commute an hour and a half each way, every day to her job in Davis – that she hated. After three years of this, she told me she finally decided to sell the condo because the commute really was killing her. I could not have been happier for her, until she told me what she planned to do with the money she would clear from the sale.

"Now I can get a place closer to work."

I almost fell over. In the seven years she's had this job, I've never heard a single story of it providing a moment's joy. She is a mid-ranking, in-house accountant for a major manufacturer, and she is going to use the half-million dollars that she now has in the bank to *move closer to work*.

"Or you could quit," I said. The conversation continued and I learned more. In addition to the money from the home, she had cashed in some stock options and had an additional $450,000. She was also still getting several thousand dollars a month in alimony.

Even though she had nearly a million dollars in the bank, I could not convince her to quit the job she hated. So I tried to get her to take a one-year sabbatical. Her reply: "What if they replace me while I'm gone and I can't go back?"

"Then don't go back!" I cried.

That notion was lost. Her Fear of not being able to get another job kept her from leaving the one she hated. She has 16 years of exceptional experience, enough money to live on for the rest of her life at a level that will keep her as comfortable as her current lifestyle, and absolutely no desire to do what she's doing every single day. It's maddening to me.

We met working on a deal when I was practicing law, and she and her husband had just moved to San Francisco from Chicago because her husband was offered a partnership in one of the Big Five accounting firms. She had loved Chicago – never wanted to leave, and still tells me how much she wishes she could go back there. Of course, in this real estate market, she could buy an amazing condo on the Gold Coast for cash, and still have half a million dollars to live on. So why isn't she doing this? Fear.

I asked her if she's ever made a decision in her life based on what will make her happy, but I knew the answer. Her father and brother never allowed her a moment of childhood that wasn't about them; then, at 17, she met the man she married (at 21), who required everyone in his sphere to orbit around him like he was the sun. Making decisions based on what would make her happy, as opposed to what would keep her safe, or cause the least disturbance, would be as foreign to her as speaking Greek. She is simply not capable of doing it naturally.

We had a long conversation this past weekend. She was very excited to tell me about the new house she just closed on. In Davis, California. Only 15 minutes from work. I forced back tears as I lied and told her how happy I was for her.

If I had one wish for this woman it would be that she have some giant shock to the system that causes her to re-evaluate everything – her own equivalent of my February 11th, and that she comes through it deciding that her decisions can be motivated by what will make her happy. Not Fear. Not expectation or obligation or "the norm," but simply what she wants.

Remember, once you start in Motion, it's easy to stay in Motion. Then allow yourself the Satisfaction that comes with it. Now, ditch the Fear. These simple nouns are all that's standing between you and being truly happy.

CHAPTER

8

THE ADJECTIVES OF HAPPINESS

I n the original outline for this book, there was no
chapter covering the adjectives in Happiness, but
when a girlfriend was talking recently about why she
has no success with men, she said, matter-of-factly, "I'm
sure it's because my dad never told me I was pretty."

On the page, that may look like a joke, but to this
woman, it's a painful memory of something she needed
that she never got. That started me thinking about how
the adjectives we use to describe ourselves (and how
others see us) can increase or decrease our happiness.

For me, "pretty" was never a problem. I am the younger
of two sisters and it was always, "Carol's the smart one and
Valerie's the pretty one." I had no need to convince people I
was pretty and never put any effort into it, because every day of

my childhood and beyond, I was told how pretty I was. What I was not told was how smart I was. This turned me into an intolerable, obnoxious blowhard with a constant need to show everyone how smart I was – to always prove that I was always right (even if no one was disagreeing with me).

I came by it naturally, of course. It was the language my father spoke. As my grandfather used to say to him on a daily basis, "You'd rather be right than President." The need to be right was his gift to me.

Luckily, I was blessed by God with an even greater gift, more valuable than being smart or pretty, and that is self-awareness. At various points in my life, I've had the chance to get a glimpse of how others perceived me – the adjectives they would use to describe me, and often I didn't like the picture, which I have always taken as an opportunity for a little Motion. If you look at yourself and don't like the view, change it.

One of my greatest blessings came from a classmate I clashed with regularly in college. We were in the same campus organization, but on opposite sides of every issue. If I wanted red, she wanted blue, and so on for three years. One day, at a meeting, we got into a literal screaming match, after which I stormed out furious, and wrote her an angry letter about everything she was wrong about. Her reply did not address a single one of my issues with her.

Instead, it was all about the ways I was sabotaging myself with my behavior. To start with, she told me I was one of the smartest people she'd ever met (WHAT??!!) and if I would just listen to other people and work with them, my ideas would get better, not overridden.

I no longer have the letter (I desperately wish I did), but I'll never forget her last line. She wrote, "If you would just try to be a member of this club, rather than always needing to be its leader, you'd find that everyone would follow you anyway."

That woman saved me from my worst self. Without her words to make me see what I needed to do to be who I wanted to be, I don't think I ever would have been able to find the true happiness that sustains me every day.

As soon as I finished reading it, I went to find her and thank her. Even then, I knew a sea change was coming. She told me that she had really worked hard not to be angry while she was writing it, and that she cared more about keeping me as a friend (WHAT??!! She thinks of me as a friend?) than about being right.

I see her only at organized reunion events these days, but every time it reminds me how much she did for me with the one simple act of writing me an honest letter.

So what adjectives do you need to feel happy? More importantly, what are you doing to <u>be</u> those adjectives, and are you able to hear them when they are applied to you? My friend who thinks she is so unsuccessful with men because her father never told her she was pretty, does nothing to make herself pretty.

I'm not saying that's what women need to do to be happy, but if not being told you're pretty makes you unhappy, do something about it. Get a nice haircut. Put on a little makeup. Buy some cute clothes. More importantly, when people tell you that you look pretty, be willing to hear it.

On two occasions when she has dressed up, I've told her how beautiful she looked, and she immediately disagreed with me. Once, we were with another friend (an actress who is quite attractive), and my friend replied to my compliment about how pretty she was by saying, "No one's going to look at me with Amy around." That made me sad. It's not Amy who is making her feel unpretty, it's her.

Try this: write down the five adjectives you NEED to believe about yourself and/or need others to think describe you. This will be the start of an important Motion, but it requires total, brutal honesty. If you need others to see you as creative, what are you creating? If you need others to see you as compassionate, what compassion – real, true compassion – have you brought to the world?

Don't beat yourself up over what you aren't doing, or aren't "being." The reason this chapter comes so late in the book is because it's hard work. By now you should be getting proficient at Respecting yourself and Releasing the thoughts and feelings that make you unhappy, and hopefully you have constant Motion from which you get genuine Satisfaction. So now, you need to decide how you want the world to see you, what you want people to think and feel about you, and what you will do to get there. Then, as you start to become what you want to be, Reward yourself (because this is a BIG deal) – you are well on your way to sustained, permanent happiness.

My five adjectives are:

1. Gracious
2. Intelligent
3. Funny
4. Successful
5. Beautiful (yes, I want people to think this about me)

Number one (gracious) is the hardest, because it doesn't come to me naturally. In my youth, I experienced a lot of Schadenfreude (the joy at others' misfortunes) and angrily begrudged people who had more than I did.

It is only with self-awareness and vigilance that I've turned this around and am on my way to becoming truly gracious. Learning to be kind in this way is probably my proudest achievement, as it is the one thing I always knew I should be, even in my most ungracious moments. I'm not sure if it's one of the first things people say about me now, or if it would even occur to them to say it at all, but at this point in my life, it is something people no longer would disagree with (which was not always true).

Number two (intelligent) actually is not a problem, as long as I can keep my mouth shut about it long enough for people to come to that conclusion naturally.

Number three (funny) is just a matter of paying very close attention to people who are naturally funny (or seem so) and figuring out what works and what doesn't, in terms of timing, wordplay and wit. Trust me, you can teach yourself to be funny – you just have to work at it.

Number four (successful) is a never-ending quest. It is the one area I cannot afford to be at all stagnant, and probably the one I am most insecure about.

When I was discussing this chapter with my friend Naomi over coffee, she couldn't believe I felt that way about my own success, and she said, "But you're so accomplished." (As you'll remember, this is the same thing my cousin Heidi told me.)

You see, there's the difference. To me, accomplished is not the same as successful, and I need to be seen as successful.

How many people can you think of who have starred in movies, won national championships or set world records and are now in drug rehab or bankrupt? Those people are very accomplished, but are they successful? For me, there are certain benchmarks I have to achieve to think of myself as successful, and I simply haven't reached them yet. They may change over time, but that quest keeps me in motion, and of course, Motion is required for happiness.

It turns out, as I age, number five (beautiful) is no longer a given, and something I am slowly coming to grips with. As someone who is not a fan of unnecessary medical procedures (and exceedingly anti-pain), it's likely that I will age the way the starlets of old did – gracefully (God willing) and naturally, and if that makes me less physically attractive than in my earlier days, I will just chalk that up as the price of greater wisdom.

Still, I like being told now and then that I'm hot. It doesn't happen the way it used to, so maybe I value it all that much more. The good thing is, as I write this, I realize that my happiness does not hinge on this word, so pretty soon I'll probably Release it and find something more valuable to add to my personal adjectives list.

❄❄❄

But back to you! What are your five adjectives? On a later page is an assortment of all the personal adjectives I could think of that people may want to be, or to have others think of them.

DON'T PEEK! Try to come up with your five first (don't let my list influence you), but then use my list to hone yours to perfection. Think very hard about this.

Do you want people to think you are smart...or wise? Intelligent or knowledgeable? Pretty, beautiful, hot or attractive? Use the subtle differences in what those words mean to you to pick the right ones. Choose carefully, then, Motion, my friend...Motion.

My Five Adjectives:
1.
2.
3.
4.
5.

Now check your list against the possibilities on the next page. Is there something there that you didn't think of, but which means more to you? Go ahead and swap it out. Is there a more specific word than the one you chose? The importance of this work is to be completely honest with yourself about what you want to be in order to be happy, so striving for something that isn't an exact fit works against you.

Also, if you only have three on your list, that's fine. It's about your happiness, and if that gets you there, then that's all you need.

Smart	Wise	Intelligent	Knowledgeable
Pretty	Beautiful	Hot	Attractive
Influential	Powerful	Intimidating	Expert
Strong	Effective	Independent	Organized
Talented	Creative	Constructive	Interesting
Entrepreneurial	Broad-Minded	Impulsive	Fearless
Mysterious	Respectful	Healthy	Assertive
Aggressive	Analytical	Perceptive	Vocal
Adventurer	Risk-Taker	Outspoken	Personable
Reserved	Worldly	Curious	Diplomatic
Resourceful	Practical	Optimistic	Efficient
Dynamic	Imaginative	Logical	Brave
Punctual	Serious	Calm	Trustworthy
Faithful	Loyal	Nurturing	Strong
Eclectic	Offbeat	Weird	Free-Spirited
Spiritual	Religious	Pious	Humble
Modest	Friendly	Gracious	Open
Quiet	Funny	Hilarious	Crazy
Devilish	Social	Frugal	Economical
Thoughtful	Reliable	Realistic	Goal-Oriented
Self-starter	Kind	Charming	Inspirational

Continued on next page...

Insightful	Compassionate	Generous	Passionate
Loving	Affectionate	Easygoing	Playful
Outgoing	Hospitable	Sympathetic	Pleasant
Forthright	Candid	Emphatic	Honest
Athletic	Gentle	Fierce	Irresistible
Witty	Entertaining	Sparkling	Wealthy
Lucky	Blessed	Worthy	Special
Unique	Notable	Memorable	Sweet
Dedicated	Patriotic	Agitating	Demanding
Sexy	Soulful	Seductive	Romantic

This is by no means an exhaustive list, but if you can be totally honest with yourself, not only whether others see you this way, but whether you truly are working to be described by the five words you chose, then you will be on your way to lasting, permanent happiness.

CHAPTER

9

THE NEGATIVE FORM IN HAPPINESS

Je suis heureux – "I am happy."

Je ne suis pas heureux – "I am not happy."

There will always be people on the planet who will want to negate your happiness – to add the "negative form" to your phrasing. There is nothing you can do to change them; the only thing you can do is change how you absorb and react to them.

Direct Negators

Direct Negators are people who will try to reduce your happiness. When being told about, or simply perceiving, how happy you are, they will launch the attack. It might be overt ("You're actually happy that your son got a B in calculus? He won't get into a good college with a B on his record"), but it is far more likely to be insidious and sneaky ("He finally got a B in calculus? How nice. He should get into a decent state school, now.")

Below are some examples of things a Negator might say in the face of your happiness:

1. "But being promoted to Assistant Manager still doesn't get you health benefits, does it?"

2. "Doesn't this car [...your new car that you love...] get really bad gas mileage?"

3. "You and John getting together just proves that there's someone for everyone."

4. "Wow, I could never travel by myself, without my husband. It's great that you've adapted to being single and are so adventurous."

5. "It's a sweet dog. I prefer purebreds, myself."

Now, it is the most natural of human reactions to engage in this behavior and defend your newfound happiness, but there is no upside in that. The Negators are trying to throw you off your game, but they can't do that because you are no longer speaking the same language. You speak Happiness, and since that's the language you respond in, the conversation will likely end there, and you can go on to a topic on which you do speak the same language.

But how do you respond to the above attacks in Happiness? Try these on for size:

1. *"But being promoted to Assistant Manager still doesn't get you health benefits, does it?"* REPLY: "I'm so happy about this promotion, I'm not going to focus on things like that." If the Negator pushes and tries to get you to reply in his language, smile sweetly and say, "Thanks so much for your concern. Hey, how are things going with the house remodel/your new sales territory/your son in rehab?"

2. *"Doesn't this car get really bad gas mileage?"* REPLY: "Probably. I won't know until I've driven it ten or twenty thousand miles, and I am going to LOVE those miles." If the Negator is terribly concerned about your effect on the planet and won't let it go, smile sweetly and say, "I know what you mean. The technology really should have advanced by now. That reminds me, I've been reading a lot about wind power, lately. What do you think? Can it work?"

3. *"You and John getting together just proves that there's someone for everyone."* REPLY: "Thank you! I agree, we are so much in love. I've never been happier."

4. *"Wow, I could never travel by myself, without my husband. It's great that you've adapted to being single and are so adventurous."* REPLY: "Yes, it is. (HUGE smile when you say this) So, where was the last place you and your husband went?"

5. *"It's a sweet dog. I prefer purebreds, myself."* Just smile sweetly and walk away.

Here's the important thing about all of the above replies, spoken in fluent Happiness – they aren't defensive. You do not have to defend your happiness to anyone else, and getting ensnared in such a conversation will only cause you to get confused and revert to your native language.

When faced with a Direct Negator, give yourself a moment to translate your thoughts into Happiness, thank them for their concern and/or praise (no matter how faint) and change the subject back to them. Negators are unhappy, and they are just looking forward to speaking Unhappiness to someone who will listen.

Indirect Negators

Indirect Negators are people whose own unhappiness is so palpable that it risks becoming contagious. The Indirect Negator is the person who bitches, moans, goes off on a rant, gets on a soapbox, or just generally spews negativity, but you still want to have a relationship with, or are stuck dealing with due to work or family obligations.

This is not to say that people have to be cheerful all the time. You don't, and Lord knows, I'm not. Also, to be a true friend, you have to be able to hear and absorb your friends' complaints on occasion and provide thoughtful advice, an ear to bend, or just a shoulder to cry on, whichever is needed.

But when you think about a person who is best described as a "whiner" or a "done-to" (i.e., everything is always done to them) how do you maintain your happiness in their presence? It's easier than you think.

First, don't get sucked into the conversation. Sometimes, one person can go on and on without the other having to contribute. It's tiring, but it is far less tiring than finding yourself complaining about something that doesn't really bother you, or didn't until the Negator came along.

My own worst experience with this was having lunch with a friend who was having severe marital problems. As we got into the third hour of our lunch (no, I'm not exaggerating), I found myself trying to join the conversation with tales of my own marital woes. The thing is, I really didn't have any marital woes, so I was taking little annoyances about my spouse (that weren't really an issue for me anyway) and conflating them into bigger problems so that I could "relate" to her.

I didn't need to relate to her, and she didn't need me to relate to her, so what was the point? I drove away from that lunch feeling sick to my stomach that I had said such ridiculously stupid things, and worse, that she would think that my marriage was less wonderful than it was. The next time we spoke, I tried to clarify how great things were with my husband, but by then it was too late. She'd heard what she heard. I was so angry at myself that I had to put that one in my Release file and let it go, but I made sure to learn from my mistake.

What I learned was a mental trick that I am now passing on to you. The friend who taught me this trick is a psychic reader. She is not a scam artist, and whether you believe in that sort of thing or not, the point is that she and her clients believe in it, so she follows a number of techniques to prepare herself for a reading, one of which is "raising her energy shields."

Before she engages with someone, she mentally forms an invisible shield between herself and that person, so that she can "read" them without absorbing their energy into her own. I realize that to many people this sounds like a lot of New Age babble, but just try it.

Next time you are faced with someone ranting about getting a parking ticket, or having to pay too much for a new roof, or the undesirable people moving into her neighborhood, silently say to yourself, "Energy shields UP!" then picture an invisible, unbreakable glass wall forming between the two of you. You can still hear their words, but their negativity will bounce right off the wall, back at the other person. You don't absorb, you don't engage, and you don't let your happiness get negated. You'll actually feel your happiness grow, almost palpably, at the thought that you are not being brought down.

I recently went to an entertainment industry event that I was very excited about, until I ran into an acquaintance who is a classic "done-to" and he decided to sit at our table. As he was going on and on about being the only person at the company to get laid off from his latest job and how he was going to sue, I felt the muscles in my neck start to form knots, then I remembered that I don't have to absorb his energy. I took a deep breath and thought "energy shields UP!" and within moments, I felt the tension drain out of my body. He had no way of knowing I was blocking his negativity in that way, but I kept my happiness intact.

Are YOU the Negator?

One other way we inhibit our own happiness is to diminish the happiness of others. Sometimes you don't even realize you're doing it, but if you are – STOP. You have an obligation to become self-aware in this area and, whether you can fix the root problem for yourself or not, prevent yourself from Negating, as that is a sure-fire block to your own happiness.

There were two languages spoken in my home growing up that led to me being a negator. My mother's language was Begrudgement and my father's was Be-Right-ment.

When my mother was a girl, there was never enough in her home. Never enough money, never enough food, and sadly, never enough love. As a child in that environment, she became very self-deprivational, and also developed the belief that people who had a lot didn't deserve it. Even in her own hard-fought success, she has never been able to just spend money freely on herself, never really seeing her own "deservingness."

Because this was one of the languages spoken in my home, it wasn't until my early twenties that I began (just barely) to see things differently. I had to teach myself not to begrudge rich people their wealth, especially if I someday wanted to be financially successful, and I had to learn that I deserve what I've got, even some of the extravagances.

That has not always stopped me from being critical of what my friends have bought, or what they've spent, which has never been my business in the first place. If I found out that someone's bills were paid by their parents or a trust fund, I judged that they didn't deserve what they had. I had no respect for them, and let it show. This is an uphill battle for me to this very day.

However, when I was 22, I had a lucky encounter that made me see what I wanted to be in this regard. My mom took me, her mother, her sister-in-law and her best friend on a cruise. (You see, she is able to spend money on herself, as long as it's for other people, too.) Since I was the youngest single person on the boat by at least thirty years, I spent the entire trip hanging out with the band who had been brought on just for that sailing, a country singer named Michelle Wright and her back-up musicians. We had a ball, and on the last day at sea, we all went to the giant final bingo tournament.

Michelle was playing multiple cards, whooping and hollering and having a great time (as we all were), but she was also intent on winning. When it came down to the final game of the cruise, a cover-all that seemed to take forever, she was one number away from shouting "Bingo!" and walking away with the $2000 grand prize when we heard it from across the room.

An elderly man had gotten a bingo first. He worked his way to the stage, and we all sat in anticipation as they verified his card, then announced it was official. He was the winner. To me, all our time and money had been wasted, but then Michelle turned around and said to me, "How great for him!" and she meant it with all her heart.

After sitting next to her, watching her very real competitiveness for over two hours, I was astonished. To be able to lose and be genuinely happy for the winner was as foreign a language to me as Swahili, but right then, I knew I wanted to speak it. To this day, I play hard, but go home happy, win or lose, and for the most part, happy for the person who won as well. That has freed me to be happy for people who have things I don't have (like a new car, a trust fund, or the ability to spend money on themselves guilt-free) and the ability to desire their fortune without begrudging it. Thank you, Michelle.

As discussed in Chapter Eight, the legacy from the other side of my family was a need to prove I was right, in any given situation. My father would rather "be right than President." He didn't care who he alienated, hurt or angered, as long as they had to concede that he was right.

I, too, spent years striving to "Be Right," before seeing how that need was contributing to my own unhappiness as well as that of the people around me.

Now, I'm generally content to nod and say, "Wow, I didn't see it that way," and let it go, and surprisingly, the outcome is almost always better. Even on factual things that I can easily prove, I rarely insist on correcting the other person, unless the world will end or puppies will die if I don't.

Of course, sometimes I don't even catch that I'm in Be Right territory until it's too late. This very morning, before I got to the computer to type, I had a "Be Right" moment that I wish I could take back.

My husband came to bed last night cracking up over a message that a friend of his had left on our answering machine. Convinced that his friend was drunk, calling from a party, he saved the message for me to listen to. The next morning, after I heard it, I told him that the friend wasn't at a party, it was the TV on in the background, and he wasn't drunk, he'd just lost his train of thought. My husband disagreed, so I insisted that he play the message again. I was even able to tell him what show was on in the background.

After carefully listening, he shrugged and said I was right, but that his way was funnier. As I watched him trudge down the hall to his office, it occurred to me that he had really enjoyed that message last night. He could have giggled about it to himself for days, and since he's not the type who would tease a friend about something like that, or repeat it to anyone else, no one else would have ever known that he thought his friend drunk-dialed us from a party. So I'm kicking myself today for taking a little of the joy out of his life for nothing. And knowing I did that makes me less happy. I should remember, it's better to be Wright (i.e., Michelle) than Right.

Are you sabotaging your own happiness by taking happiness away from other people? Here's a good test. Spend a week being really observant in all of your interactions. As you walk away, does the person you were just with seem happier, or unhappier, having spoken with you? Do you feel you added or subtracted joy from their lives? Is this an encounter both of you would want to repeat? Be honest with yourself.

And one big tip – if other people start telling you you're a Negator, even if they're not fluent speakers of Happiness and thus use different terminology, don't get defensive. Pay attention. Ask for specific details and focus on areas where you can improve. Remember, being a Negator is no different than being attacked by a Negator; it reduces your fluency in Happiness.

Exercise:

Did you meet a Negator today? Were you a Negator today? If so, here are some possible entries for your Count-to-Five list:

❈ I'm happy that when Joan tried to negate my happiness, she didn't succeed.

❈ I'm happy that I spotted the negativity in Mark's comments today and didn't get sucked into arguing with him or defending myself.

❈ I'm happy that I stopped myself from making a critical comment about Alison's new hair color. She seemed so happy with it and I didn't want to negate that.

❈ I'm happy that Bob asked me not to roll my eyes whenever he talks in meetings. (Always happy to get feedback!) I don't need to negate him to make myself feel better, and I'd rather contribute to global happiness than take away from it. I still think he's an idiot, but I can keep that to myself. I plan to work on being more positive in my interactions with him from now on.

CHAPTER
10

HAPPINESS – PAST, PRESENT AND FUTURE TENSE (AND "FUTURE UNCERTAIN")

I am happy.
I was happy.
I will be happy.
I might be happy in the long run.

Every language has an algorithm for talking about what is happening right now (in the present tense), what happened yesterday (past tense) or what will happen tomorrow (future tense). This is one of the more complex things to learn in a new language, because for every rule, there are a dozen or so exceptions that you have to memorize to be conversant in the language. The same is true for Happiness.

Some guidelines about Past and Future Happiness will seem to be in direct contradiction with other things in this book (like actively Remembering things you did that made you happy), but they are the exceptions. The rules here are simple: don't let the happiness that you had (or lacked) in the past be what determines how happy you are now, and don't anticipate future happiness (that may or may not materialize) to offset present misery.

Past Tense

Past happiness can be your greatest asset or your greatest liability in achieving lasting, permanent happiness. Past unhappiness can be your greatest asset or your greatest liability in achieving lasting, permanent happiness. You have to learn how to use your past as a guidepost, but not a crutch. It can be a learning experience, but not the chain that holds you back.

When we studied Verbs, it was important to learn that when you are feeling lousy about yourself, you should stop and think about what you've done in the past that made you happy. It could be an act as tiny as cutting down a plant that's blocking your view, or as enormous as saying "I do" to the person you love, but it had to be something you did that gave you happiness.

Then you use that memory to give yourself a little boost of happy in the present.

This is a very effective technique, but it should only be used as a pick-me-up during the lulls. It cannot be your main source of joy, for many reasons. First, you don't live in the past, so only getting your happiness from the past takes away the opportunity to be happy in the present. If you are looking back on past situations (particularly past loves) as having made you happy, and comparing them negatively to where you are today, chances are very good that they weren't anywhere near as rosy in reality as they are in your memory, and you are making today worse by creating the negative comparison. An ex is an ex for a reason, whether it's an ex-job or an ex-lover or an ex-home. It wasn't right at the time, and looking back as if it was doesn't make it so.

Second, only thinking about when you were happy *back then* is likely to make you more dissatisfied with wherever you are now. Think of it this way – if you only drove your car by looking in the rear-view mirror, you would have a very hard time getting anywhere. You do need to glance into the mirror now and then to keep your journey going smoothly, but it can't be your main focus. Looking back for happiness is the same thing. The occasional glance is fine, but keep your eyes focused ahead.

The other danger of living in the past is if it was particularly *unhappy*, and that hurt shackles your ability to experience joy. Do you do this to yourself: every time you get close to being happy, you flash back to something bad or wrong that you did (or that someone did to you) and ruin the moment? Go back to Chapter Six and get a refresher in Releasing the thoughts that keep you unhappy. Don't let the past control you in the present. Release.

However, if you suffer from this kind of constant drain on your emotions, then Releasing may not be enough. Ask why you do this to yourself. Why do you allow some act or slight from the past to block you like a linebacker every time you get close to happy? This may be some tough work, but start with, "I have no reason not to be happy and every right to be happy, so what makes me punish myself in this way?" Try really hard to answer that question.

If, in your past, someone has hurt you in a way that makes you feel unworthy of happiness, take that hurt out of you and beat the living crap out of it. I am not kidding. Sometimes to Release anger and hurt and fear, we need to do it physically, and let me tell you – Walmart sells piñatas for under ten bucks.

This is not a joke. Go buy a piñata and fill it with all the rewards of happiness that you long for, but block yourself from. Write notes on index cards, buy little gifts for you, think of treats that you enjoy and put them in there (or some representation of them – you can't put a doughnut in a piñata, but you can put in a gift card for your favorite doughnut shop).

You can do this in an afternoon, or you can fill it over days or weeks, but when the time is right, find a place to hang your "past hurt" piñata, then really focus on making yourself see what it represents. This object is the physical form of an event from your past that is keeping you from being happy. Want to reclaim your happiness? Stand back – no blindfold necessary - and beat the living daylights out of it.

With each swing, Release the hurt, Release the pain, Release blaming yourself, Release hating someone else. Don't forget – this does not require forgiveness, it simply requires you to physically feel that *thing* which is holding you back departing from your body, and the result will be a shower of rewards, literally, as you break through and get what you've been wanting all along.

Are there people in your life on this journey with you? Invite them. Have a piñata party. Unless one of them is being represented by your piñata. That person does not belong there. You do not need for them to know that they've caused you all this pain in order for you to release it, and in fact, I promise you – I GUARANTEE – having the person you hold responsible for your unhappiness know that you feel that way will NOT release you from it. In fact, it will probably make it worse.

Remember – this is about YOU. It is about your happiness. You have to release your need for an apology, or an explanation, or restitution. Once you no longer need those things, you can be on your way to happiness, and surprisingly, the apology or the explanation may come anyway, out of the blue. But your needing it only hurts you – it does not hurt the person you need it from, and honestly, why hurt yourself?

Once again, I know this is hard work. So is learning the past tense construct of any new language, but you can't be fluent unless you do it. Past happiness is good as a nice reminder, but should not be the joy you cling to at the expense of happiness today, and past unhappiness cannot be the hook that pulls you back every time you are close to what you want.

Present Tense

Happiness in the present tense is about distinguishing between permanent happiness and situational happiness. Permanent happiness is what this book is geared towards. It is about changing your state of being to become a happy person. It is as much a part of who you are as the language you speak.

Permanent happiness means that regardless of your situation, you can still have Motion and Satisfaction. You still actively Respect, Remember, Release and Reward, you are still described with the adjectives you aspire to. You can end every day counting at least five things that made you happy, and after tracking your good days and your glum days for a while, you've noticed how many fewer glum days you have. You noticed a particular color in two or three different places and that gave you a smile. In the present, you are happy.

Situational happiness is the kind of happiness that only occurs when all the planets align in the way you want them to. It's easy to be happy when everything is going your way. It's effortless when all your dreams have come true and you tell yourself you're happy, but if undoing any or all of that takes away your happiness, then in the present, you are not yet happy.

I used to have a terrible pattern in relationships (before I spotted it and made life much easier on the men in my life thereafter). When I was single for a time, I would go through phases of being happy and phases of being unhappy. It was like a wave that ebbed and flowed, and I rode it out. Old souls call it having The Blues, and when you've got the blues, there are a few things you can do – sing about 'em, ignore 'em, wallow in 'em, or get your body moving and shake 'em off. The point is, it's a natural part of life to get the blues. I even believe it's chemical. It happens.

The problem is, when I was in a relationship with someone, and those same emotional lows hit, instead of thinking, "Yep, sometimes I'm just unhappy," I looked at that other person and thought, "You're making me unhappy." Depending on the relationship, we could ride one or two of those swings out, sometimes even more, but it always ended eventually, because each time I felt more and more resentment at whatever it was this person was doing to make me so unhappy. Believe me, when you're with someone, and you're grouchy, you can always find a dozen things they're doing wrong.

When it finally hit me that no one was making me unhappy other than me (and the alignment of the planets), it became quite easy to ride out the blues, even with another person in the picture. You can't imagine how powerful it is to say to the person who loves you, "I've got the blues right now, and I'm kind of a grouch (or I'm kind of sad), so if you don't mind, I just need to wallow in it until it goes away." Or, "I need you to help me make it go away."

Give them the freedom to acknowledge your foul mood, without getting blamed for it, and they'll be much more understanding. The flip side is, this should not be a weekly occurrence, and if you truly love that person (and respect yourself), you'll work really hard (meaning do all the work in this book) to prevent it from happening more than once or twice a year. Truly happy people want to be surrounded by other happy people (it's like learning a foreign language by immersion), so allow others to be happy being around you, and be happy around them.

Future Tense

How many people do you know who are waiting for some outside thing to happen so that they can be happy?

They are banking on happiness in the future...if only "X" would happen. If I move out of this city. If I get a better job. If I win the lottery. If I get a date with Carla. If I break up with Jim. If I could afford those cute shoes. If I had a nicer car.

What they have is situational unhappiness. They are looking at where they are, not undertaking any Motion towards happiness, and just waiting. For what? Beats me. Because here is the secret: once they get whatever it is, it still won't make them happy.

Future happiness is solely the result of becoming fluent in Happiness in the present. Are you happy now? Do you have permanent happiness, with all the requisite nouns and verbs? If so, keep doing what you are doing and you will be happy in the future.

Are you unhappy now? Then you need Motion. You need to go back to Chapter One and figure out how to introduce yourself as a happy person. Let me ask you something – did you read this book in one day? Heck, you may have read it in a couple hours. If that's the case, then it didn't work for you. It can't. This is not a beach read, it's a textbook. You have to master the chapters one at a time. It takes work.

I'm teaching myself to play the piano right now. I have never had any music lessons and have absolutely no innate musical talent, and guess what? IT IS SO MUCH WORK!

Learning to read music is basically learning a new language, and when you are over forty, it's not the same as when you were under ten. It feels as if my brain is actively resistant to absorbing the information. So I plug away a little at a time, every day, because being able to play this instrument is my goal. I did not sit down, read the Beginning Piano book start-to-finish and assume that meant I would know how to play.

Slamming through this book cover to cover like some speed reading exercise will not help you achieve your goal of lasting, permanent happiness. Neither will winning the lottery. Do the work. One chapter at a time. Until you can honestly answer whenever someone asks how you are with: "I'm happy."

Future Uncertain Tense

There is one more verb tense to study, unique to the language of Happiness, and that is the Future Uncertain Tense. The basic construct in this tense is that you have no way of knowing whether a miserable situation today will lead to greater happiness in the future or not. There are a few exceptions in cases of extreme devastation, but for the general rule, you don't know, so don't leap to any conclusions.

Can you look back on something bad in your life, that in hindsight turned out to be the best thing that ever happened to you? Was there a time when you didn't get that job you really wanted, or the love-of-your-life broke up with you, or some minor annoyance caused you to change your plans, that later proved unconditionally fortunate? How many women do you know who seemed destroyed when their husbands left them and are now the happiest they've ever been?

Garth Brooks has a song that includes the lyrics: "Sometimes I thank God for unanswered prayers." Think about how many things you've wanted that you didn't get, and later discovered that life was much better that way.

In addition to February 11, 2000, going from being the worst day of my life to being among the best (as described in the opening chapter), I have two other stories from my own life to make this point, and they are the reason I never let bad news or unexpected losses infringe on my core happiness. Because the truth is, I don't know what the universe might be planning for me, and it might be better than what I've planned for myself.

The first glaring example of "hindsight happiness" occurred from 1989-1995. In 1989, entering my senior year of college, I got the shock of my life when my advisor, the chair of Trinity University's economics department, informed me that he would not be writing a letter of recommendation for me to go to an economics graduate program (the path I had been striving for since sophomore year) and that no other economics professor would either.

His theory was that with my grades and GRE scores, I would get into any program I applied to, but with a huge hole in my education regarding advanced math, I would fail out. (I had dropped out of both Calculus III and Matrix Algebra the previous year.) Since Trinity is so small and only sends maybe one or two candidates to a Ph.D. program in any given year, my failure would harm any subsequent candidates from our school.

I could not believe it. All I wanted was to become an economics professor and here I was being told that that door was closed to me. This is pretty tough for a 20-year-old to process.

In the meantime, I had been teaching prep classes for the LSAT (the Law School Admissions Test) since my junior year for a company called The Princeton Review, and that fall, they forced me to take the test, so I would have an official score on record. They even paid me my regular hourly rate to take it. Bottom line: teaching prep for two years and not caring about the outcome of the test can lead to a pretty good score, and my grades were geared towards getting into a Ph.D. program, so you can see where this is going.

With no desire to go to law school or be a lawyer, but with few other prospects, I applied to four schools, got in to all four, and went to Berkeley Law – because it didn't snow there.

I HATED it, and dropped out after the first year to apply for econ Ph.D. programs. Luckily, I got into the

Environmental Economics department at Berkeley, and upon their request, re-admitted to the law school so that I wouldn't count in their budget and they could admit another student as well.

To make a long story short, being an economist wasn't for me, so after I completed my Masters, I finished law school (in 1995, right at the start of the dot-com boom), and had a stunning career as an IPO lawyer, venture capital consultant, investment banker and Internet executive, none of which would have happened had Dr. Butler written me a glowing recommendation for an economics graduate program. That was one of those situations where not getting what I wanted turned out to be a very, VERY, good thing. (And on a side note – the math in my econ grad program *kicked my butt!* Had I not had a year of law school and a year of working in the real world to learn how to really knuckle down and tackle something that hard, I would have failed out...exactly as Dr. Butler had predicted.)

❅❅❅

A more somber event in my life took place on July 4th, 1998, and is the reason I never complain about the little annoyances that might disrupt my otherwise meticulously planned schedule.

That night, my friend Doug and I decided to go to the Alameda County Fair to catch the 6:00 p.m. Peter

Frampton concert and then afterwards walk around the midway to eat, play carnival games, ride rides, etc.

The day before, I had had some dental work done and the hygienist nicked my lip, which had now turned into a festering wound. When Doug picked me up, I told him I wouldn't be able to eat most of the food at the fair because of my wound, and, being the great friend he is, he insisted that we find a drugstore near the fairgrounds where I could get some Kanka to cover it up.

This took nearly half an hour, and by the time we got to the fair, the parking lots were full and we had to find street parking. I was extremely cranky, not only about my sore lip, but also because we had missed the start of the Frampton concert. Turns out, this was no big deal, he was playing again at 8:30, so Doug and I hit the booths and the midway and planned to be in the concert up until the fireworks.

About 45 minutes into the show, we heard popping noises that sounded like the fireworks might have started early, and saw people running from the midway - the very place we would have been at that moment had I not had the wound on my lip and had we not had to search for parking on the street. Moments later, police came into the arena and shut down the concert.

We would find out hours later that while we were in the concert, a 22-year-old gangbanger had run into rival gang members in the midway and opened fire on the crowd, hitting nine people. Another dozen were injured in the ensuing stampede.

Amid the confusion, we found our way back to the car, which was thankfully parked on the street, but not before noticing that the parking lot had turned into lawless chaos, as people desperately tried to get their families out of the area while gang members ran among the vehicles, hopping on hoods and throwing bottles at windshields. Several fights broke out.

Even as I type this, I am shaking remembering the overwhelming insecurity I felt that night. We were 100% safe, and removed from all of the violence, but when I think about what could have been – where we were supposed to be had all gone according to plan - I have to take a deep breath and thank God for things like careless dental assistants and small parking lots and friends who are flexible with their plans.

❋❋❋

We do not know what the future holds. Do not let your happiness be dictated by your current circumstances. I was devastated when I found out I wasn't going to graduate school for economics, but in hindsight, I wouldn't change a thing. How many events in your past is that true of?

Sometimes the rewards come years later. If my first managers in Hollywood hadn't been so horrible, I never would have met my husband. If my mother hadn't had a brain tumor (from which she is 100% recovered), I never would have become a screenwriter. If any number of boyfriends hadn't turned out to be the wrong fit, I never would have had the exciting careers I've enjoyed, as I probably would have stayed with one of them, moving to whatever locale best served his dreams. The most important thing to remember about the Future Uncertain Tense of Happiness is that when speaking it, we simply don't know what the results will be.

Next time you can't find a parking spot, or miss a plane, or have your plans hindered by someone else's ineptitude, before you get mad, remember that this could be the best thing that ever happens to you. You might never know it, and it could create all kinds of disasters instead, but keeping the possibility of endless upside in mind will always make you happy.

CHAPTER

11

KEY PHRASES IN YOUR NEW LANGUAGE

"¿Dónde está el baño?"

S ome of the first things you learn in any new language are a few common phrases to help you navigate the territory if you find yourself needing to speak it.

There are thousands of phrases that have been coined since the beginning of time to help you get by when first learning to speak Happiness. You may already know several of them. A few are collected below.

Pick your favorites and memorize them. Share them with others. Put them on post-it notes at your desk or inside your wallet, just as little reminders of your new language, until you are fluent.

You may not agree with all of them. Feel free to ignore those that will not help you learn your new language, and add any that you're familiar with that may not be included here. This collection is not comprehensive – it's just a starter set. Enjoy!

❉❉❉

In every life we have some trouble. When you worry you make it double. Don't worry, be happy...

Bobby McFerrin

Happiness is the meaning and the purpose of life, the whole aim and end of human existence.

Aristotle

You just have to do your own thing, no matter what anyone says. It's your life.

Ethan Embry

Each moment of a happy lover's hour is worth an age of dull and common life.

Aphra Behn

Success is not the key to happiness. Happiness is the key to success. If you love what you are doing, you will be successful.

Herman Cain

The reason people find it so hard to be happy is that they always see the past better than it was, the present worse than it is, and the future less resolved than it will be.

Marcel Pagnol

If you want to live a happy life, tie it to a goal, not to people or things.

Albert Einstein

It isn't what you have, or who you are, or where you are, or what you are doing that makes you happy or unhappy. It is what you think about.

Dale Carnegie

Happiness always looks small while you hold it in your hands, but let it go, and you learn at once how big and precious it is.

Maxim Gorky

To me, there are three things we all should do every day. We should do this every day of our lives. Number one is laugh. You should laugh every day. Number two is think. You should spend some time in thought. And number three is, you should have your emotions moved to tears, could be happiness or joy. But think about it. If you laugh, you think, and you cry, that's a full day. That's a heck of a day. You do that seven days a week, you're going to have something special.

Jim Valvano

Thousands of candles can be lit from a single candle, and the life of the candle will not be shortened. Happiness never decreases by being shared.

Buddha

Some cause happiness wherever they go; others whenever they go.

Oscar Wilde

Most folks are about as happy as they make up their minds to be.

Abraham Lincoln

The secret of happiness is to make others believe they are the cause of it.

Al Batt

Happiness is nothing more than good health and a bad memory.

Albert Schweitzer

Contentment makes poor men rich; discontentment makes rich men poor.

Benjamin Franklin

If there were in the world today any large number of people who desired their own happiness more than they desired the unhappiness of others, we could have paradise in a few years.

Bertrand Russell

All I can say about life is, "Oh God, enjoy it!"

Bob Newhart

The foolish man seeks happiness in the distance, the wise grows it under his feet.

James Oppenheim

I've grown to realize the joy that comes from little victories is preferable to the fun that comes from ease and the pursuit of pleasure.

Lawana Blackwell

Happiness isn't something you experience; it's something you remember.

Oscar Levant

No man is happy who does not think himself so.

Publilius Syrus, Maxims

Make one person happy each day and in forty years you will have made 14,600 human beings happy for a little time at least.

Charles Wiley

When you finally allow yourself to trust joy and embrace it, you will find you dance with everything.

Emanuel

To live long and achieve happiness, cultivate the art of radiating happiness.

Malcolm Forbes

Perceive and rejoice that life is abundant, that beauty and goodness are amply available...that your happiness is in your hands.

Paul Hodges

Happiness does not consist in things, but in the relish we have of them.

Francois, Duc de la Rochefoucald

Enjoy your life without comparing it to others.

Condobcet

The true secret of happiness lies in taking a genuine interest in all the details of daily life and elevating them to an art.

William Morris

We tend to forget that happiness doesn't come as a result of getting something we don't have, but rather of recognizing and appreciating what we do have.

Frederick Koenig

Happiness is not the absence of problems; but the ability to deal with them.

Jack Brown

*It was only a sunny smile and little it cost in the giving
but like morning light it scattered the night
and made the day worth living.*

F. Scott Fitzgerald

Some pursue happiness, others create it.

A fortune cookie I got last week

APPENDIX
WHAT THIS BOOK
DOES NOT COVER

This book is in no way intended to replace professional counseling where needed. If you are experiencing overwhelming unhappiness as a result of grief, substance abuse or a chemical imbalance, this book may provide you with temporary relief and some useful insights, but it is crucial that you seek out and continue with some type of professional help.

Grief

Grief is the beast that you cannot tame. The emotional reactions we deal with in the face of loss are varied and all over the map, and cannot be relegated to taking "a few days to get over it," as some around you might suggest. If you need to grieve - grieve. It's a healthy process, and to suppress it will only delay the inevitable.

Everyone is familiar with the concept of "five stages of grief" – Denial, Anger, Bargaining, Depression and Acceptance – but most people believe that these occur in order, one-by-one, until they run their course. Nothing could be farther from the truth.

These emotions, and the multitude of others that accompany grieving, are like a deck of cards that has been shuffled repeatedly. You never know which one (or two or three) will hit you, sometimes all at once, and sometimes years after the loss that triggered them.

Here is the important thing to remember about grief: it diminishes over time. I can't say that it passes, because for some people, it never does. But as long as grief isn't taking over your life, allow yourself the freedom to grieve your loss, and don't allow others to dictate the boundaries of your grief.

I was blessed that the first time I suffered a real loss, my neighbor (whose husband had died several years earlier) sat on my front porch for hours and told me what to expect, how to recognize good, old-fashioned grief when it sneaks up on me, and how to embrace it, get through it, and go on. To this day, I am enormously grateful to her, and this is what I grieve, unapologetically:

❈ My grandmother was one of my best friends in the world, and even though she died over ten years ago, I still have moments of missing her deeply and feeling sorry for myself that she's not around. I can't believe she'll never meet my husband. Man, she would have loved him – and vice versa.

❄ I lost a dog a few years ago that had been my closest companion for nearly 13 years, and even though I now have a husband, a new dog, and a plan to start a family soon, on occasion, something will remind me of Jasmine and I'll find myself crying.

❄ I did not know a single person who died in the World Trade Center, but even typing those words makes me well up in tears. I can't see the New York City skyline without feeling a twinge of real loss.

All of the above is grief. Very real, deeply felt, and not within my control. I find my happiness outside my grief, but I'm fortunate that I can. I haven't lost a parent, a spouse or a child, and I know that if and when I do, grief will hit a whole new level. I hope I am prepared for it, but until then, I would never tell another person that I understand what they are going through, because I don't. Everyone's grief is their own unique experience.

In the face of loss, however, you may also find yourself surrounded by well-meaning idiots. Basically, when someone dies, the great majority of people have no idea what to say, and sometimes get it really (really!) wrong. There are two good phrases for all situations when speaking to a person who has lost a loved one:

1. I am so sorry for your loss; and

2. I don't know what to say, but please let me know if there is anything I can do to help.

Aside from these, people are treading on dangerous ground, which means that you, the grief-stricken one seeking to someday regain your fluency in Happiness, have to remember to forget. As discussed in Chapter Six, Release is one of the verbs of Happiness. If someone makes a boneheaded comment at your darkest hour, try to remember that they were there to make it, which means that they love you and wanted to comfort you. Release them from the burden of having somehow hurt you and release yourself from carrying around that pain. (On a side note, the phrase, "Everything happens for a reason" is never, <u>EVER</u> appropriate to say to a parent who has just lost a child. That sentiment has plenty of other places in life where it fits, but not there.)

If a loss has become overwhelming for you, seek real help. There are a variety of choices, from therapists to professional grief counselors to support groups for those who have suffered a similar loss. You can find these resources on the Internet, through a local house of worship or hospital, and even in the Yellow Pages.

Do not try to go through this alone. And never forget that happiness will return to your life, hopefully sooner rather than later.

Substance Abuse

Unlike grief, substance abuse is the beast that you can tame, and while you may not be able to overcome your addiction alone, it is within your control to seek assistance. Now is the perfect time to find a counselor, a support group or a clinic that can help. Why now? Because you are reading this book, which means that you are actively seeking happiness, and permanent happiness (as opposed to situational happiness, as discussed in Chapter Ten) is not possible when your life is controlled by drugs or alcohol.

In her book, "I'll Scream Later," actress Marlee Matlin revealed that she was in the Betty Ford Clinic the day her Oscar nomination was announced. It would seem that she should have been one of the five happiest women on the planet at that moment, but that extraordinary achievement wasn't enough to make her happy, because she had an addiction. I include her story here because, at the time, she actually equated the drugs with happiness, as many users do.

In her own words, "I could never stop thinking about drugs. If I didn't have a joint that day...I wouldn't be a happy person, if I didn't have my coke I wouldn't be a happy person. Nothing made me happy except the drugs. That's how bad it was."

Drugs and alcohol will NOT make you a happy person. They can temporarily relieve pain, but when they wear off, the pain is still right there, and chances are, it's grown. The most important thing to remember is that drugs and alcohol are not the cause of your unhappiness, they're a symptom. And if your unhappiness is so great that you've turned to a chemical substance to alleviate it, it is time to get professional help. This book will not get you there. I should know, I wrote it.

Mental Illness and Chemical Imbalance

I feel quite unqualified to talk about this topic, having never been faced with the prospect of not having control of my mental and emotional faculties; however, it has to be addressed here as an illness which causes great unhappiness and which a book like this one cannot heal.

If you believe that your emotional state is outside of your control, and that this is a chronic problem affecting you and those around you, please seek a competent mental health professional in your area to give you an accurate diagnosis and begin a course of treatment.

It's okay to ask a lot of questions. It's okay to demand an "exit strategy" for when you might be able to reduce the dosage of your meds or get off them entirely. It's okay to get a second opinion. In fact, get several.

It is not okay to let it go untreated and potentially become a danger to yourself and others. Happiness is within your realm of possibilities, you just have to work much harder for it, and for that, I am so sorry. I wish you the best of luck getting to the place where something as simple as counting five things each day that make you happy can provide the same permanent happiness for you that it can for others.

AFTERTHOUGHTS

D id you actually try telling people you're happy, as instructed in Chapter One? Did you get some strange responses? If you think that was tough, you can just imagine the replies you get when telling people you're writing a book about happiness. Most of them sound something like, "What qualifies you as an expert on THAT?"

To this, I have consistently replied, "Because I'm so happy."

This does not reduce their skepticism any, but it sure makes me happy to say it.

I will be the first to acknowledge that there are experts, many with Ph.D.s, who have done multiple clinical studies on what makes human beings happy, and I'm sure their findings are quite compelling, but will reading those studies make a person happy? Maybe. I don't know. I do know that I have yet to meet a psychiatrist who was even remotely happy, but that's probably just me. Your mileage may vary.

Still, that fact matters. A lot of successful screenwriting books are written by people who have never sold a screenplay, and plenty of worthy cookbooks are written by people who aren't professional chefs, but in order to write a textbook on happiness, I think the author had better be truly happy, and have a cognitive awareness of how she got that way. Thus, I qualify.

I spent the first 31 years of my life being unhappy, and probably making the people around me a bit miserable, too. After a year spent in limbo (a.k.a. Indiana), where nothing was about me, but somehow I got more out of it than anyone, I decided to make a fundamental change.

I've now spent the last decade being almost deliriously happy, even when going broke, falling on my face or having my heart broken, simply because I decided that HAPPY was going to be part of my DNA.

It was not the primary language spoken in my home as a child, but by now I'm quite fluent. Hopefully, if I have children, they will be native speakers, and this new language – this aspect of their heritage – will be passed down for many generations to come.

I sincerely hope that this book helps you get to the place where Happiness is the language you speak - the dialect you dream in, the mother tongue of the company you keep and the lyrics that sustain you in your darkest hours.

Happiness is within your reach. To borrow a line from one of my favorite films: "Maybe not today, maybe not tomorrow, but soon...and for the rest of your life."

ACKNOWLEDGEMENTS

There have been so many people in my life that have contributed to my happiness, or my journey towards happiness, that it would be impossible to name them all here, so I will stick with the people who specifically helped with this book.

Many thanks to the following people: Naomi Beaty and Jan McCusker for being the first two sets of eyes to read the manuscript and give feedback. Christiana Miller and Keith Domingue for wonderful advice about publishing and promotion. My dad, Shelley Horwitz, for the unsolicited, but remarkably helpful, copy edit. And Rick Alexander, for being the best husband any writer could ask for.

A SPECIAL NOTE ABOUT MY PARENTS

When someone writes a book about having to learn how to be happy, and includes examples from her own life, it's pretty easy to make all kinds of assumptions about the people who raised her. Here's the bottom line: my parents are wonderful, loving people who have supported me through every decision I've made in life, including some that would make most parents' heads explode.

They've both read this book, and accept what I've written, but both of them remember a lot more happy times than are conveyed here, and that's fair. It's all a matter of perspective. The thing I can say with certainty about my parents is that they truly enjoyed having children, and even liked being around my sister and me, for the most part. Yes, there was emotional turbulence and things I had to figure out how to process, both as a teenager and as an adult, but I love them dearly and am deeply grateful for the many gifts they've given me. Thanks, Mom and Dad.

ABOUT THE AUTHOR

Valerie Alexander started her career in the Silicon Valley during the Dot-Com gold rush of the late 1990s, where she worked on some of the most high-profile transactions of the decade as a securities lawyer, an investment banker and an Internet executive.

From 2000 to 2001, she returned to Indiana to care for her mother, and in her absence the Internet bubble burst, leaving her no choice but to move to Los Angeles to write and direct movies.

As a screenwriter, Valerie has worked with Joel Schumacher, Catherine Zeta Jones, Ice Cube and others. Not satisfied writing scripts that never got made, she co-wrote, produced and directed the award-winning short film, *Making the Cut*, as well as numerous commercials and public service announcements.

Valerie received her B.A. from Trinity University and her J.D. and M.S. degrees from the University of California, Berkeley. In the spring of 2010, she returned to Berkeley Law to teach the legal ethics seminar, "Representation of Law in Film," and she continues to lecture at colleges and film schools across the country with her entertaining talk, "How to Survive in Hollywood (Despite Having a Female Brain)."

Valerie lives in Los Angeles with her husband, writer and producer Rick Alexander, and their ill-mannered German Shepherd, Pepper.

CPSIA information can be obtained
at www.ICGtesting.com
Printed in the USA
FSHW020045060520
69871FS